How To Play Otamatone

A Beginner's Guide To Mastering The Otamatone With 30 Songs, Techniques, And Interactive Exercises

Theo Harmonia

Table of Contents

Introduction

About the Otamatone

The Otamatone is a unique and playful musical instrument, easily recognizable by its quirky, tadpole-like design and distinctive, vocal-like sound. Created by the Japanese company **Maywa Denki** and first introduced in 1998, the Otamatone quickly captured attention with its blend of novelty and musicality. Its structure consists of a simple body and neck, resembling a note symbol, with a "mouth" that opens to create sound modulation. Despite its unconventional appearance, the Otamatone produces rich, expressive tones that can mimic the human voice, making it both entertaining and musically versatile.

The instrument operates on a sliding pitch mechanism, where the player's finger movement along the neck determines pitch, while squeezing the mouth controls volume and expression. This straightforward design offers an entry point for both seasoned musicians and absolute beginners to experiment with pitch, dynamics, and unique tonal effects.

Why the Otamatone is Fun and Accessible

One of the biggest attractions of the Otamatone is its simplicity. Unlike traditional instruments that require rigorous training and dexterity, the Otamatone's design makes it accessible to people of all ages, including young children, and requires minimal setup to start playing. It encourages immediate engagement with sound and expression, allowing users to produce melodies quickly without a deep understanding of music theory.

The Otamatone also offers expressive potential not often found in beginner-friendly instruments. Players can add vibrato, glides, and dynamic shifts simply by adjusting finger pressure and "mouth" control. The Otamatone is also portable and battery-operated, making it a great option for on-the-go playing or impromptu performances. For these reasons, it appeals to anyone seeking a fun, flexible instrument that can grow with them as their skills improve.

Chapter 1: Getting Started With The Otamatone

Parts Of The Otamatone

Understanding the parts of the Otamatone will help you navigate the instrument and start producing sound with confidence. Here's a breakdown of each key component:

1. **Neck (Slider Area)**

   o The Otamatone's neck functions similarly to a fretboard on a string instrument. Moving your finger up and down the neck changes the pitch: sliding upwards raises the pitch, while sliding downwards lowers it.

   o **Slider Mechanics:** The neck is sensitive to touch, and small finger movements make precise adjustments to pitch. It's recommended to begin with gentle slides to understand how

much pressure and movement
produce different tones.

2. **Mouth**

○ The mouth is the expressive part of
the Otamatone and opens and closes
with pressure from your hand.
Squeezing the cheeks of the mouth
changes the tone, allowing you to
control volume and add expression,
almost like a vocalist.

○ **How It Works:** When squeezed, the
mouth alters sound resonance, making
it louder or softer depending on
pressure. Practice by holding a steady
pitch with the slider while gradually
squeezing the mouth to feel how
sound changes.

3. **Power Switch**

- Located at the back or bottom of the Otamatone, the power switch turns the instrument on and off. Be sure to turn it off after each use to preserve battery life.

- **Battery Information:** The Otamatone is usually powered by AAA batteries, which should be replaced regularly for the best sound quality. When sound starts to distort or fades quickly, it may be time to change batteries.

4. **Volume Knob**

- The volume knob allows you to control the overall loudness of the Otamatone. Adjusting it will help you find a comfortable sound level depending on your environment.

- **Using Volume Effectively:**
  Beginners can start by setting the volume to a low or medium level. Experiment with adjusting the volume while playing to develop a feel for balance between pitch and dynamic range.

Basic Care and Maintenance

Taking care of your Otamatone will ensure it functions well and continues to produce high-quality sound. Here are essential tips for maintaining your instrument:

1. **Battery Maintenance**

   o Always turn off the power switch when the Otamatone is not in use to conserve battery life.

   o Remove batteries if you won't be using the Otamatone for an extended period to prevent leakage, which can damage internal components.

2. **Cleaning**

   o **Exterior Cleaning:** Use a soft, dry cloth to wipe the exterior, especially around the mouth and neck area. Avoid using water or harsh cleaning chemicals, as these could damage the surface or seep into the instrument.

- o **Mouth Area:** The mouth is an area of high use, so it may accumulate dust or smudges. Gently clean around it with a dry cloth to maintain the mechanism's sensitivity.

3. **Slider Area Care**

- o The slider is sensitive and requires clean, dry hands for smooth playability. Keep the slider free of oils or moisture from your hands, as these could affect pitch accuracy and responsiveness.

- o If the slider becomes sticky, a quick wipe with a dry cloth is usually sufficient. Avoid excessive pressure to prevent wearing out the touch-sensitive area.

4. **Storage**

  o Store the Otamatone in a cool, dry
     place away from direct sunlight and
     extreme temperatures. Excessive heat
     or cold can cause damage to internal
     electronics and affect sound quality.

  o **Carrying Cases:** If possible, use a
     carrying case to protect the
     Otamatone from accidental bumps
     and scratches, especially during
     travel.

5. **Regular Inspections**

  o Check your Otamatone regularly for
     any loose or malfunctioning parts,
     such as the mouth mechanism or
     power switch. Catching issues early
     will help you keep the instrument in
     good working condition.

- o Contact the manufacturer for repairs or replacement parts if any issues persist, particularly with essential components like the slider or volume knob.

With a basic understanding of the Otamatone's parts and maintenance, you are ready to start playing! Each component plays a role in shaping your sound, and maintaining these parts will ensure you get the most out of your Otamatone. Moving forward, you'll dive deeper into holding techniques, finger placement, and eventually learn to play your first notes and melodies.

Chapter 2: Setting Up And Holding The Otamatone

Turning It On And Adjusting Volume

Let's start by powering on your Otamatone and setting it up for optimal sound control. Here's a step-by-step guide:

1. Locate the Power Switch

- **Where to Find It:** The power switch is usually located on the back or bottom of the Otamatone's body. It may be labeled with an "ON/OFF" marking.

- **Step-by-Step Instructions:**

    1. Hold the Otamatone with both hands to locate the switch.

    2. Slide or toggle the switch to the "ON" position. You may hear a faint sound as the Otamatone powers on, indicating it's ready to play.

2. Check Battery Levels (If Necessary)

- **Signs of Low Battery:** If the sound is weak, distorted, or cutting in and out, it may be time to replace the batteries.

- **How to Replace Batteries:**

  1. Open the battery compartment, which is often found near the base of the Otamatone.

  2. Insert fresh AAA batteries, following the polarity guide inside the compartment.

  3. Close the compartment securely.

3. Adjust the Volume Knob

- **Where to Find It:** The volume knob is typically located near the power switch or on the side of the Otamatone.

- **Step-by-Step Instructions:**

1. Start by turning the volume knob to a low or medium setting. This will help prevent any sudden loud sounds when you start playing.

2. As you begin to play, you can adjust the volume based on your surroundings and preference.

   - **Tip:** For practice in quiet settings, a lower volume is ideal. For louder environments, turn up the volume as needed to hear the instrument clearly.

4. Test the Sound

- **Try Out a Few Notes:** Slide your finger along the neck (slider area) to confirm that the Otamatone is producing sound.

- **Adjust as Needed:** Listen to the sound quality and make minor adjustments to the volume knob until you're satisfied with the level.

Once your Otamatone is powered on and the volume is adjusted, you're ready to dive into basic techniques and start experimenting with different tones and pitches!

Next, let's look at the best way to hold the Otamatone for comfortable playing and control.

Proper Grip And Posture: Holding The Otamatone For Optimal Control

The way you hold the Otamatone affects your ability to control pitch, volume, and expressiveness. Here are some recommended grips and postures for different playing styles.

1. Basic Grip for Beginners

- **Purpose:** Provides stability and control, ideal for learning basic pitch and volume techniques.

- **How to Hold:**

    1. **Non-Dominant Hand (Holding the Neck):** Use your non-dominant hand to hold the neck of the Otamatone. Place your thumb behind the neck for support, and use your index or middle finger to slide along the neck to control pitch.

2. **Dominant Hand (Controlling the Mouth):** Position your dominant hand on the "mouth" area, with your fingers on one side and your thumb on the other. This allows you to squeeze the mouth easily to adjust volume and tone.

- **Posture Tips:**

  o Hold the Otamatone at chest height for easy access to both the neck and mouth.

  o Relax your shoulders and wrists to prevent strain during longer practice sessions.

- **Advantages:** This grip provides a balanced control over pitch and volume, ideal for beginners learning to manage both elements.

2. Advanced Grip for Greater Expression

- **Purpose:** Allows more nuanced control of pitch and expression, suitable as you progress.

- **How to Hold:**

  1. **Non-Dominant Hand (Slider Technique):** Rest your non-dominant hand fingers lightly on the neck, using the tip of your index finger for more precise pitch control. Practice using both up-and-down slides and small finger movements for subtle pitch changes.

  2. **Dominant Hand (Enhanced Mouth Control):** Use your dominant hand to wrap around the mouth area more firmly. Place your thumb on one side and your other fingers on the opposite side, squeezing gently to create

vibrato effects or adjust volume
dynamically.

- **Posture Tips:**

  o Keep the Otamatone close to your
    body, allowing your dominant hand to
    move freely around the mouth without
    losing balance.

  o Stand or sit up straight to maintain
    control over both hands and allow
    fluid movement.

- **Advantages:** This grip provides advanced
  control over expression, enabling techniques
  like vibrato, rapid volume changes, and
  smoother slides.

3. One-Handed Playing (For Simple Melodies)

- **Purpose:** Simplifies playing for very basic
  melodies or when focusing solely on pitch.

- **How to Hold:**

1. **One-Hand Grip:** Hold the Otamatone's neck with your dominant hand, using your thumb for support and your fingers to control pitch. For very simple notes, you can play without adjusting the mouth.

2. **Relaxed Hand Position:** Keep a loose grip on the neck, allowing easy movement up and down the slider for basic melodies.

- **Posture Tips:**

  o Hold the Otamatone vertically in front of you with a relaxed grip.

  o Ensure your wrist is loose to avoid tension, especially if you're playing for extended periods.

- **Advantages:** Ideal for beginners who want to focus solely on pitch without adding volume control, or when trying to play simplified tunes.

4. Seated Playing Posture

- **Purpose:** Adds stability for longer practice sessions and allows for more control while sitting.

- **How to Hold:**

  1. Sit with a straight back and place the Otamatone's bottom against your thigh for additional support.

  2. Use the basic grip, with one hand controlling the slider and the other controlling the mouth, as described in the beginner or advanced grip.

- **Posture Tips:**

  o Keep your shoulders relaxed and your elbows close to your body.

- ○ Position the Otamatone so that both hands can reach comfortably, allowing easy access to both the slider and mouth.

- **Advantages:** Provides additional stability and reduces hand fatigue, making it perfect for practicing techniques for an extended period.

Additional Tips for Holding the Otamatone

- **Grip Pressure:** Avoid gripping too tightly, as this can restrict movement. A relaxed grip allows for more fluid control over pitch and volume.

- **Adjusting for Size:** The Otamatone comes in various sizes. If using a larger or mini version, adjust your grip and posture as needed to comfortably reach both the neck and mouth.

- **Experiment with Positions:** As you get comfortable, try slight adjustments in grip and posture to find what works best for your playing style and comfort.

By finding a comfortable grip and posture, you'll be able to play smoothly and with greater expression. With these techniques, you're now ready to start experimenting with basic sounds and begin developing your Otamatone skills!

Finger Placement and Basic Slider Movements

To start playing the Otamatone effectively, you'll need to coordinate finger placement on the slider with mouth control. Here's a breakdown of how each hand works together to create smooth pitch changes and expressive sounds.

Finger Placement on the Slider

The slider on the Otamatone's neck functions similarly to a fretboard on a guitar, allowing you to control pitch. Here's how to position your fingers for optimal accuracy and control:

1. **Finger Choice and Placement**

   o **Use Your Index Finger**: For the most control, beginners should use their index finger to press on the slider. The index finger allows for precise placement and can easily slide up and down the neck.

- ○ **Supporting with the Thumb**: Place your thumb behind the neck for added support. This helps stabilize your grip and keeps your hand steady while sliding.

2. **Finding Notes on the Slider**

   - ○ **Pitch Changes**: The pitch increases as you slide your finger up the neck and decreases as you slide it down. Moving small distances results in smaller pitch changes, while larger movements create bigger shifts.

   - ○ **Note Locations**: Experiment with finger placement along the neck to locate notes such as C, D, E, etc. Use the center of the slider for higher notes and the base for lower ones.

   - ○ **Practice Tip**: Start with a few simple notes (like C, D, E) and practice finding them by sliding your finger into position without looking, so you can develop muscle memory for different note locations.

Basic Slider Movements

Moving your finger smoothly along the slider is key to creating connected and accurate notes on the Otamatone. Here's a breakdown of the basic movements:

1. **Sliding Up and Down the Slider**

    o **Slow, Controlled Slides**: To create smooth transitions between notes, press gently with your index finger and slide slowly from one note to the next. This produces a legato (connected) sound and makes the Otamatone's tone sound continuous.

    o **Quick Slides**: Rapid slides create a glissando effect, similar to sliding between notes on a trombone or string instrument. Practice this by moving from one note to another quickly, allowing you to play expressive effects in songs.

2. **Lift-and-Place Movement for Distinct Notes**

   o If you want distinct, separated notes (known as staccato), lift your finger off the slider briefly between each note instead of sliding continuously.

   o **How to Practice**: Place your finger on the slider for a note, lift it off briefly, then press down on a new note. This technique will be helpful when playing specific rhythms or melodies that require separation between notes.

Controlling the "Mouth" for Expression

The Otamatone's mouth allows you to add volume and expressive changes to the sound. Use your other hand to manipulate the mouth while you slide on the neck:

1. **Basic Mouth Control**

   o **Squeeze for Volume**: The mouth is controlled by gently squeezing it with your fingers. A firm squeeze increases the volume, while a light squeeze softens it.

   o **Maintaining Consistent Pressure**: For a steady sound, apply consistent pressure on the mouth while sliding your finger along the neck. This keeps the volume even and creates a clear, steady tone.

2. **Adding Vibrato**

o **Small, Rapid Squeezes**: To add vibrato (a slight wobble in pitch), try squeezing and releasing the mouth rapidly while holding a note on the slider. This will create a subtle variation in volume that mimics vibrato, adding emotional depth to your sound.

o **Practice Tip**: Hold a single note and practice varying your squeeze pressure slightly in rhythm, aiming for an even, pulsating sound.

Coordinating Both Hands: Tips And Exercises

Once you're comfortable with finger placement and basic slider movement, it's time to practice coordinating both hands for smooth, expressive play.

1. **Exercise 1: Steady Note with Mouth Control**

   o **Goal**: Hold a steady note on the slider while adjusting the volume with the mouth.

   o **Instructions**:

      1. Place your index finger on a note (like C) and hold it steady.

      2. Slowly squeeze and release the mouth to create volume variations.

3. Practice making small volume changes while keeping the pitch steady.

2. **Exercise 2: Sliding with Dynamic Changes**

   o **Goal**: Slide between two notes while adjusting volume.

   o **Instructions**:

      1. Start on a low note (such as A) and slide up to a higher note (like E) while gradually squeezing the mouth for more volume.

      2. Reverse the process, sliding back down while decreasing the volume.

3. **Exercise 3: Staccato Notes with Mouth Control**

- **Goal**: Play distinct notes using lift-and-place finger movements while adding volume control.

- **Instructions**:

    1. Place your finger on the first note, squeeze the mouth briefly, then release.

    2. Lift your finger, move to the next note, and repeat the mouth squeeze.

    3. Practice this on a simple melody (like "Mary Had a Little Lamb") to develop control over note separation and volume.

By practicing finger placement on the slider and learning to control the mouth, you'll gain essential skills in pitch and expression. This coordination will make your playing more dynamic and set the foundation for learning songs and techniques. In the next chapter, we'll start applying these skills to play simple melodies!

Chapter 3: Understanding The Basics Of Sound And Pitch

How Sound Is Produced On The Otamatone

The Otamatone produces sound through a unique combination of analog and electronic mechanisms, creating its characteristic voice-like tone. Unlike traditional string or wind instruments, the Otamatone's pitch and volume are controlled by a mix of pressure and movement on its slider and mouth. Let's explore how these elements work together to produce sound and how you can control them for different effects.

Internal Mechanisms of the Otamatone

1. **The Electronic Oscillator**

   o At the heart of the Otamatone is a small electronic oscillator, an internal component that generates sound waves when the instrument is powered on.

- **How It Works:** The oscillator converts electrical energy into sound vibrations. As you interact with the Otamatone's slider and mouth, the oscillator adjusts the pitch and volume of these vibrations, producing the Otamatone's unique, synthesized sound.

- **Sound Frequency:** Moving your finger up or down the slider alters the frequency of the oscillator, which corresponds to the pitch of the sound produced. Higher frequencies create higher pitches, while lower frequencies create deeper, lower notes.

2. **The Slider (Pitch Control)**

- The Otamatone's neck acts as a sliding touch-sensitive interface, where finger position determines the pitch.

- How It Works: When you place your finger on the slider, it sends an electronic signal to the oscillator to produce a specific pitch. Moving your finger up the slider (closer to the head) increases the pitch, while moving it down the slider (closer to the body) lowers the pitch.

- Range of Pitch: The slider has a limited range, typically covering one or two octaves, depending on the size of the Otamatone. Each position on the slider represents a different note, allowing you to play scales, melodies, and specific intervals.

3. The Mouth Mechanism (Volume and Timbre Control)

o The Otamatone's mouth is a hinged area that can be squeezed or released, controlling the volume and tone quality of the sound.

o **How It Works:** When you press the mouth area, it acts on the speaker or sound outlet of the Otamatone, amplifying the sound as the "mouth" opens and softening it as the "mouth" closes. This mimics how vocal cords or a singer's mouth shape the sound.

o **Dynamic Control:** Squeezing harder increases the sound's volume, making the tone more open and resonant. Softer squeezes create a more muted, quieter effect. This provides an expressive range, allowing you to emphasize certain notes or phrases with dynamic changes.

How Sound Varies with Pressure and Slider Placement

Understanding how pressure and slider placement interact is essential for producing clear and expressive tones on the Otamatone. Here's a closer look at each element:

1. **Pitch Variation through Slider Placement**

   o **Sliding Up and Down**: Moving your finger up the slider toward the Otamatone's head increases the pitch, while moving it down lowers the pitch.

   o **Finding Specific Notes**: Each point along the slider represents a different note. As you become familiar with where each note is located, you'll be able to slide to specific pitches accurately, which is essential for playing recognizable melodies.

2. **Volume and Expression through Mouth Pressure**

- ○ **Changing Volume**: By squeezing the mouth more or less, you control how loud the sound is. Stronger pressure makes the sound louder and fuller, while lighter pressure softens it.

- ○ **Creating Vocal-Like Effects**: The mouth pressure lets you add expression similar to a singer's voice. For example:

  - **Vibrato**: By rapidly varying the pressure on the mouth while holding a pitch, you can create a vibrato effect, adding warmth to your sound.

  - **Legato and Staccato**: To produce legato (smooth) notes, keep steady pressure on the

42

mouth while moving along the slider. For staccato (short) notes, briefly press and release the mouth for each note.

3. **Combining Pitch and Volume for Dynamic Expression**

   o To achieve expressive phrasing on the Otamatone, practice coordinating your slider movements with mouth pressure. For example:

      ▪ **Crescendo and Decrescendo**: Start on a lower note and increase pressure on the mouth while sliding up the slider for a rising, swelling sound. Reverse the process for a gradual fade or decrescendo.

      ▪ **Phrasing and Emphasis**: In a melody, use extra mouth

pressure on important notes for emphasis, and lighten pressure on connecting notes for smoother transitions.

Practice Exercises for Sound Control

To get familiar with how the Otamatone produces sound and how to control pitch and volume, here are a few exercises:

1. **Exercise 1: Basic Pitch Control on the Slider**

    o **Goal**: Practice moving between notes smoothly.

    o **Instructions**:

        1. Place your finger on a low note near the base of the slider.

        2. Slide up slowly, listening to the gradual increase in pitch.

3. Try to land on specific notes (such as C, D, E) by adjusting your finger placement.

4. Repeat, moving both up and down the slider to develop a feel for each note's location.

2. **Exercise 2: Volume Control with Mouth Pressure**

   o **Goal**: Develop control over volume and dynamics using the mouth.

   o **Instructions**:

      1. Hold a steady note on the slider (any note you choose).

      2. Gradually increase pressure on the mouth to make the sound louder, then gradually release to soften it.

3. Repeat, trying to create even increases and decreases in volume.

3. **Exercise 3: Combining Pitch and Volume**

   o **Goal**: Coordinate slider and mouth movements for expressive play.

   o **Instructions**:

      1. Choose a simple pattern, such as moving from a low note to a high note and back down.

      2. Start quietly, increasing the volume as you slide up to the higher note, then softening as you slide back down.

      3. Experiment with different speeds and pressure combinations to explore the Otamatone's expressive range.

Pitch and Tone Control: Achieving Precise Pitches on the Otamatone

To play melodies accurately on the Otamatone, it's essential to understand how to control pitch and tone precisely. The slider on the Otamatone's neck is where you'll create different pitches, similar to the way a violinist finds notes on a fretless neck. With practice, you'll be able to locate pitches accurately and control tonal effects to create expressive sounds.

Understanding the Slider and Note Placement

The Otamatone's slider serves as a touch-sensitive area for pitch control. Unlike traditional fretted instruments where specific locations produce fixed notes, the Otamatone's slider requires careful positioning to achieve each pitch. Here's how the slider generally corresponds to musical notes:

1. **Slider Range and Octave Coverage**

   o The slider has a limited pitch range that typically covers one or two octaves, depending on the size of your Otamatone.

   o **Higher Notes:** Moving your finger up toward the head of the Otamatone produces higher pitches.

   o **Lower Notes:** Sliding your finger down toward the body results in lower pitches.

2. **Relative Note Positions**

   o Since there are no visible markers on the slider, learning the approximate locations of notes is crucial. Beginners can start by identifying the approximate positions of basic notes like C, D, E, F, G, A, and B.

- Practice Tip: Memorize the locations of these notes by frequently moving your finger from one to another, noting the distances needed for each interval. With time, you'll develop a "mental map" of the slider for finding notes more easily.

Tips for Achieving Precise Pitches

Achieving precision on the Otamatone takes practice due to the lack of fret markers, but here are some techniques to help you play accurately:

1. **Use a Light Touch and Listen Carefully**

   - Light Pressure: Apply gentle but steady pressure with your index finger to allow easy sliding. This will help you feel small movements along the slider.

   - Listen Closely: Pay close attention to the pitch changes as you move along the slider. Developing an ear for these changes will allow you to make quick adjustments when notes are slightly off.

2. **Start with Short Slides**

   o Instead of moving quickly between notes, start by sliding slowly to feel the pitch increase or decrease smoothly. This helps with tuning your ear to the pitch changes and lets you make small corrections.

   o **Exercise**: Slide from a lower pitch to a higher pitch slowly, trying to match the exact pitch of familiar notes. For instance, slide from C to G, listening carefully as you move.

3. **Use Your Finger as a "Stop"**

   o Once you locate a note, mark the position in your mind. Practice landing your finger directly on this position repeatedly to develop muscle memory.

- o **Exercise**: Choose a note (like D) and repeatedly find it on the slider, lifting and placing your finger each time to build accuracy.

4. **Fine-Tune with Small Adjustments**

- o After placing your finger on a note, you may need to make micro-adjustments to hit the exact pitch. Move your finger slightly up or down until you reach the precise tone.

- o **Exercise**: Pick a note like E, place your finger on the slider, and practice fine-tuning the pitch by making tiny adjustments until it sounds accurate.

Controlling Tone for Expressive Playing

In addition to pitch, controlling the tone quality of each note will add depth to your playing. Here are some ways to vary tone on the Otamatone:

1. **Using the Mouth for Volume and Timbre**

   o **Opening and Closing the Mouth**: Squeezing the mouth more tightly amplifies the sound and makes it brighter, while a gentle squeeze produces a softer, mellower tone.

   o **Expressive Techniques**: Use rapid, subtle squeezes while holding a note to add vibrato, giving the tone a vocal-like quality.

2. **Sliding for Smooth Transitions**

   o To create a smooth, connected sound between notes (legato), slide gradually from one note to the next without lifting your finger. This is especially useful for melodies that require a flowing, continuous sound.

- o **Exercise**: Practice sliding from C to E and back without lifting your finger to create a seamless sound.

3. **Adding Staccato and Dynamics**

- o To play distinct, separated notes (staccato), briefly lift your finger off the slider between each note. This technique is useful for rhythmic songs or emphasizing specific notes.

- o **Exercise**: Play a simple melody like "Mary Had a Little Lamb" using staccato by lifting your finger between notes.

Developing Pitch Accuracy through Exercises

With regular practice, these exercises will help you improve your pitch accuracy on the Otamatone:

1. **Exercise 1: Octave Practice**

   o **Goal**: Learn to find the same note in different octaves on the slider.

   o **Instructions**:

      1. Locate a note, such as C, near the bottom of the slider.

      2. Slide up to find the higher octave of the same note (C).

      3. Repeat, alternating between the two positions to improve your octave accuracy.

2. **Exercise 2: Scale Practice**

   o **Goal**: Practice playing scales to memorize note positions and develop a smooth slide.

54

- **Instructions**:

  1. Start with the C major scale: C-
     D-E-F-G-A-B-C.

  2. Play each note slowly,
     adjusting your finger if the
     pitch is slightly off.

  3. Repeat the scale multiple times,
     aiming for precise notes with
     each attempt.

3. **Exercise 3: Familiar Melody by Ear**

   - **Goal**: Practice pitch accuracy by
     learning a simple melody by ear.

   - **Instructions**:

     1. Choose a familiar melody, such
        as "Twinkle Twinkle Little
        Star."

     2. Attempt to play the melody on
        the slider without visual

references, using your ear to match pitches.

3. Adjust as needed, developing both your pitch control and ear training.

Practice Exercise: Moving Up and Down the Scale with the Slider

Objective

This exercise will help you develop control over pitch accuracy and tone consistency as you slide up and down a scale. You'll practice maintaining steady, even tones on each note, a key skill for playing clear, recognizable melodies on the Otamatone.

Instructions

1. **Choose a Scale**

   o Start with a simple scale, such as the **C Major scale** (C-D-E-F-G-A-B-C).

This scale includes no sharps or flats, making it easier to learn the positions of each note on the slider.

2. **Find the Starting Note (C)**

   o Begin by locating the **C** note on the slider, which is typically near the lower end (close to the body).

   o Place your index finger lightly on this position and apply gentle pressure.

3. **Moving Up the Scale**

   o **Slide to the Next Note (D)**: Keeping steady pressure, slide your finger up a small distance to reach the next note in the scale, D. Listen carefully to ensure you're hitting the correct pitch.

   o **Continue the Scale**: Progressively slide up the slider to each subsequent note in the C Major scale:

- E, F, G, A, B, and finally the higher C.

  - **Focus on Tone**: For each note, aim to produce a clear, steady tone without any wavering. Avoid sudden jumps or jerky movements, which can lead to pitch inconsistencies.

4. **Holding Each Note**

   - **Even Duration**: Try to hold each note for about two seconds before sliding to the next. This will help you practice sustaining even tones and develop a sense of timing.

   - **Adjust as Needed**: If a note sounds off-pitch, make a small adjustment by sliding your finger slightly up or down until the pitch is correct.

5. **Returning Down the Scale**

o After reaching the higher C, reverse the process by sliding back down the scale.

o **Control Your Descent**: Move slowly and smoothly from one note to the next, maintaining steady pressure to avoid abrupt sound changes.

o Repeat the sequence several times, aiming for both pitch accuracy and consistent tone with each attempt.

Tips for Success

- **Listen Closely**: Use your ear to gauge each note's pitch. If it sounds slightly sharp or flat, adjust your finger placement gently.

- **Steady Pressure**: Applying consistent pressure along the slider helps avoid any unintended changes in pitch or volume.

- **Focus on Smooth Transitions**: As you slide between notes, aim for a seamless sound with no breaks. Practicing this will improve your legato playing technique.

Expanding the Exercise

Once you're comfortable with the C Major scale, try applying this exercise to other scales, like **G Major** or **F Major**. Practicing various scales will help you build a mental map of different note positions on the slider and improve your overall control.

By practicing this exercise regularly, you'll strengthen your ability to play accurate pitches with steady tones, forming a strong foundation for playing melodies on the Otamatone.

Chapter 4: Playing Simple Melodies

Finding Notes On The Otamatone

Understanding where common notes fall on the Otamatone's slider is key to playing simple melodies. The slider layout varies slightly between Otamatone models, but the general positions of the notes are consistent:

1. **Basic Note Locations**

   o **C Note**: Found near the bottom of the slider (closer to the body).

   o **D Note**: Slightly above C, about a finger's width higher.

   o **E Note**: A bit further up from D, roughly halfway between C and G.

   o **F Note**: Near the center of the slider.

   o **G Note**: A bit above F, often at the mid-point of the slider.

- **A Note**: Higher up from G, close to three-quarters of the way up the slider.

- **B Note**: Slightly above A.

- **High C Note**: Near the top end of the slider.

2. **Practice Finding Notes**

- Start with C, then slide up to each note slowly. Repeat until you can accurately locate each note on the slider without looking.

- **Tip**: For beginners, marking approximate positions with small stickers (that don't leave residue) can help you identify notes more easily as you practice.

First Simple Songs: Step-by-Step Instructions

Let's apply your note-finding skills to some familiar melodies. Each song includes step-by-step finger placement and slider movements.

1. "Twinkle Twinkle Little Star"

- **Notes to Play**:
  - C C G G A A G
  - F F E E D D C
  - G G F F E E D
  - G G F F E E D
  - C C G G A A G
  - F F E E D D C

- **Step-by-Step Instructions**:

1. **Start on C**: Place your finger near the bottom of the slider to play C. Play it twice.

2. **Slide to G**: Move your finger about halfway up the slider to find G. Play G twice.

63

3.   **Slide to A**: Move slightly higher from G to play A. Play it twice.

4.   **Return to G**: Slide back down to G and play it once.

5.   **Continue the Melody**: Repeat the same process, following the note sequence above.

- **Practice Tip**: Go slowly, focusing on hitting each note accurately. Repeat until the melody sounds smooth.

2. "Mary Had a Little Lamb"

- **Notes to Play**:
  - E D C D E EE
  - D DD E G G
  - E D C D E EE
  - E D D E D C
- **Step-by-Step Instructions**:

1.   **Start on E**: Place your finger on the position for E, roughly halfway up the slider.

2.   **Move to D**: Slide slightly down to D, which is just below E.

3.   **Slide to C**: Move further down to find C, closer to the bottom of the slider.

4.   **Continue the Melody**: Follow the note sequence, sliding up and down between C, D, E, and G.

- **Practice Tip**: This melody has more frequent slides. Practice moving smoothly between notes to maintain a steady rhythm.

3. "Happy Birthday"

- **Notes to Play**:

  o G G A G C B

  o G G A G D C

  o G GG E C B A

o   F F E C D C

- **Step-by-Step Instructions**:

1.   **Start on G**: Find the G note about halfway up the slider. Play it twice.

2.   **Slide to A**: Move up slightly to A and play it once.

3.   **Return to G**: Slide back to G.

4.   **Move to C**: Slide up higher to reach C.

5.   **Play B**: Slide slightly down to B.

6.   **Continue the Melody**: Follow the sequence, practicing the transitions between notes.

- **Practice Tip**: This song has a few larger jumps between notes, like from G to C. Practice these jumps slowly to improve accuracy.

Practice Exercise: Playing the Major Scale and Familiarizing with Finger Positioning

Playing the major scale is an effective way to strengthen your understanding of note locations and finger positioning. Here's a simple exercise to practice moving through the scale:

1. **Choose the C Major Scale**

   o The C Major scale (C-D-E-F-G-A-B-C) is a good choice for beginners, as it uses all natural notes without sharps or flats.

2. **Step-by-Step Scale Practice**

   o **C**: Start at the bottom of the slider.

   o **D**: Move up a finger-width to D.

   o **E**: Slide up slightly further to E.

   o **F**: Move closer to the center of the slider to reach F.

   o **G**: Slide up a bit further to G.

- A: Go higher up the slider to A.

- B: Slide a small distance further to reach B.

- High C: Move to the top area of the slider for high C.

3. **Repeat the Scale**

- Go up and down the scale slowly, aiming for a smooth transition between notes.

- **Focus on Tone**: Try to hold each note for a steady two counts, maintaining an even volume and clear tone.

Tips for Effective Practice

- **Listen Closely**: Pay attention to pitch accuracy on each note. Adjust your finger position if a note sounds slightly sharp or flat.

- **Consistent Tone**: Focus on producing an even sound by applying steady pressure on the slider and mouth.

- **Repeat Regularly**: Practicing scales and simple songs daily will reinforce muscle memory, making it easier to locate notes accurately.

With these simple melodies and scale exercises, you're developing essential skills in pitch accuracy, finger positioning, and rhythm. In the next chapter, we'll dive deeper into expressive techniques to help you add dynamics and emotion to your Otamatone playing!

Chapter 5: Developing Expression And Technique

Playing the Otamatone with expression adds depth and personality to your melodies.

1. Controlling Dynamics: Adjusting Volume with the Mouth

The Otamatone's "mouth" allows you to vary volume by squeezing or releasing pressure, similar to how a singer controls volume with breath. This adds emotional impact to your melodies, helping you emphasize certain notes or phrases.

- **Increasing Volume**:
  - To make the sound louder, squeeze the mouth firmly. This opens the Otamatone's "mouth" wider, amplifying the sound.
  - **Practice Tip**: Play a simple melody, like "Mary Had a Little Lamb," and

increase the volume on specific notes to make them stand out.

- **Decreasing Volume**:
  - To soften the sound, release the pressure on the mouth slightly. A gentle squeeze creates a quieter, more muted tone.
  - **Practice Tip**: Start at a high volume, then gradually reduce pressure on each note as you play down the scale. This creates a "fade-out" effect, useful for soft endings.
- **Adding Emphasis with Dynamic Changes**:
  - Use volume changes to add emphasis and variety within a melody. For example, make the first note of a phrase louder to give it more weight, then play subsequent notes more softly.

- Exercise: Play "Twinkle Twinkle Little Star," making each "Twinkle" louder and each "little star" softer. This contrast will add dimension to the melody.

2. Adding Vibrato: Techniques for Expressive Tone

Vibrato adds a slight wobble or fluctuation in pitch, mimicking the natural vibrato of the human voice. This can add warmth and emotional expression to your playing.

- **Finger Vibrato on the Slider**:
  - Place your finger on a note and press down lightly.
  - Quickly shake your finger back and forth on the slider, moving slightly up and down from the main pitch. This will create a subtle pitch variation.

- Practice Tip: Start on a single note like G and apply vibrato by moving your finger in a small, quick motion. Try to keep the vibrato even for a smooth effect.

- **Mouth Vibrato**:
  - Instead of moving your finger, try creating vibrato by gently squeezing and releasing the mouth repeatedly.
  - This method gives a more pronounced vibrato effect by slightly altering the volume rather than pitch.
  - **Exercise**: Hold a long note like F and practice "pulsing" the mouth with gentle squeezes for a rhythmic vibrato effect.

3. Smooth Transitions Between Notes: Sliding for Connected Sounds

Smooth transitions, or "legato" playing, make melodies sound fluid and connected. To create smooth slides, avoid lifting your finger between notes and instead glide along the slider.

- **Basic Sliding Technique**:
  - Start on a note, such as C, and slowly slide your finger up the slider to reach a higher note, like G.
  - Focus on maintaining even pressure and avoiding sudden changes in pitch.
  - **Practice Tip**: Try sliding between every note in the C Major scale (C-D-E-F-G-A-B-C) without lifting your finger. This will help you develop a smooth legato technique.
- **Controlling Speed of Slides**:

- Practice both slow, gradual slides for longer, expressive transitions and quicker slides for short melodic runs.
- **Exercise**: Slide from C to E slowly, then back from E to C quickly. Try this in different sections of the scale to develop control over slide speeds.

Interactive Exercise: Varying Volume and Pitch with "Mouth" Control

This exercise will help you combine volume control, pitch accuracy, and dynamic expression, allowing you to build a strong foundation in expressive playing.

1. **Starting Note and Initial Volume**:
   - Begin on the C note at a medium volume. Use a light squeeze on the mouth to produce a clear, steady tone.
2. **Practice Gradual Volume Changes**:

- While holding the C note, slowly increase pressure on the mouth to create a crescendo (gradual increase in volume).
- After reaching a high volume, gradually reduce the pressure to return to a softer sound, creating a decrescendo.

3. **Adding Pitch Variation**:
   - Slide up to E from C while maintaining a steady volume. Focus on keeping a smooth connection between the notes.
   - Once on E, add vibrato by gently pulsing the mouth or slightly moving your finger up and down.

4. **Dynamic Melodic Phrasing**:
   - Play a short melody like "Happy Birthday," and practice adding volume emphasis to important notes, such as "Hap-" and "-day."

- Apply vibrato to the last note of each phrase for a warm, expressive ending.

5. **Combining Smooth Slides with Volume Control**:
   - Start on C, slide up to G while gradually increasing volume, then slide back down to C with a soft fade-out.
   - This practice will help you master the combination of pitch, volume, and smoothness in transitions, creating a polished, expressive sound.

Chapter 6: Introduction To Rhythm And Timing

1. Counting Beats And Maintaining Rhythm

Rhythm is the pattern of sounds and silences in music, defined by a steady pulse called the **beat**. In most songs, beats are organized into groups of four, which is known as **4/4 time**. Each count (or beat) gets an even amount of time, and maintaining this steady rhythm will help you play smoothly and keep in sync with other musicians.

- **Counting in 4/4 Time**:
  - **1, 2, 3, 4**: When counting in 4/4 time, you'll count each beat as "1, 2, 3, 4" and then start over. Each number represents a quarter note.
  - Practice tapping your foot or lightly clapping along with the counts. Keeping a steady beat while counting

aloud is the foundation for rhythmic accuracy.

- **Basic Rhythm Patterns**:
  - **Quarter Notes**: In 4/4 time, each quarter note (1, 2, 3, 4) gets one beat.
  - **Half Notes**: A half note lasts for two beats (1–2 or 3–4). Clap on "1" and hold until "3" to practice a half note.
  - **Whole Notes**: A whole note lasts for all four beats. Clap once on "1" and hold it until the next count of "1" to practice a whole note.
- **Practice Exercise**:
  - Tap out a rhythm pattern using a combination of quarter, half, and whole notes. For example: **quarter, quarter, half, quarter, whole**. This will build your comfort with different note durations and help develop timing accuracy.

2. Using a Metronome

A **metronome** is a tool that provides a steady beat, helping you keep a consistent rhythm while practicing. Most metronomes allow you to set the tempo, measured in **beats per minute (BPM)**. Starting at a slower tempo (e.g., 60 BPM) can help you focus on timing accuracy, then you can gradually increase the speed.

- **Step-by-Step Guide to Using a Metronome**:
    1. **Set the Tempo**: Begin with a slow tempo, around 60 BPM. This will give you enough time to move between notes and focus on rhythm without rushing.
    2. **Listen to the Beat**: Before playing, listen to the metronome for a few beats to get comfortable with the pace.

3. **Count Along**: Count "1, 2, 3, 4" along with the beat of the metronome. This helps sync your internal sense of timing with the metronome.

4. **Play Along with the Beat**: Start by playing a simple scale or melody, aiming to strike each note in time with each beat of the metronome.

5. **Adjust Tempo Gradually**: Once you feel comfortable, gradually increase the tempo in small increments (e.g., 70 BPM, 80 BPM) to improve speed and timing accuracy.

- **Tip**: Many metronome apps and devices allow you to set different time signatures. Set it to 4/4 to match the typical rhythm structure in beginner songs.

3. Exercise: Play Short, Timed Phrases with a Metronome

Practicing with a metronome will reinforce your timing skills. Here's a step-by-step exercise to help you build timing accuracy on the Otamatone:

1. **Choose a Simple Phrase**
   o Start with a short, familiar melody, such as "Mary Had a Little Lamb" or a basic scale.
   o Choose phrases that contain quarter, half, and whole notes to practice rhythm variation.
2. **Set the Metronome to 60 BPM**
   o Begin with a slow tempo to focus on accuracy rather than speed.
   o Listen to the beat for a few moments, then start playing along with the metronome.
3. **Play Each Note in Time**

- For quarter notes, play one note per beat (e.g., "Mary Had a Little Lamb" played as E, D, C, D in sync with "1, 2, 3, 4").

- For half notes, hold each note for two beats. In "Mary Had a Little Lamb," for instance, play E for "1–2" and D for "3–4."

- For whole notes, hold each note for all four beats.

4. **Repeat the Phrase, Increasing Tempo Gradually**

- Once you can play the phrase comfortably at 60 BPM, raise the metronome to 70 BPM, and repeat the phrase.

- Increase the tempo by 10 BPM intervals only when you feel accurate at the current speed. Aim to reach a comfortable tempo around 90 BPM.

5. **Practice Variation**

- Vary the rhythm by playing some notes as staccato (short and detached) and others as legato (smooth and connected) while still following the beat.
- **Example**: Play "Mary Had a Little Lamb" with each "Mary" note short (staccato) and "Little" note smooth (legato). This adds rhythmic dynamics to the melody.

Additional Rhythm Exercises for Accuracy

To further improve your timing, try these exercises with the metronome:

- **Rhythmic Clapping Exercise**:
  - Set the metronome to 60 BPM and clap along, counting each beat out loud. Start with quarter notes, then practice clapping on every other beat

84

(half notes) and finally on every four beats (whole notes).

- **Accent on Different Beats**:
  - Play a simple melody, such as "Twinkle Twinkle Little Star," but emphasize a different beat each time.
  - For instance, accentuate the first beat in the first phrase, then the third beat in the second phrase. This helps you build flexibility in maintaining timing while varying the emphasis.

Chapter 7: Mastering Common Songs

Song 1: "Jingle Bells"

"Jingle Bells" is a festive, easy-to-play song with a simple, repetitive melody that's perfect for beginners on the Otamatone. This melody provides an excellent opportunity to practice timing, rhythm, and smooth slides between notes, making it a joyful addition to your repertoire.

Notes and Phrases

- **Phrase 1**: E E E
- **Phrase 2**: E E E
- **Phrase 3**: E G C D E
- **Phrase 4**: F F F F F E E E E D D E D G

Fingering Instructions

Each note corresponds to a specific position on the Otamatone slider. Here's where to locate each note and how to transition between them smoothly:

- **C Note**: Near the lower end of the slider, close to the base.
- **D Note**: Slightly above C, requiring a small upward slide.
- **E Note**: Above D, in the lower-middle section.
- **F Note**: Just above E.
- **G Note**: Around the middle of the slider.

Step-by-Step Instructions for Each Phrase

Phrase 1: E E E

1. **Start on E**: Place your finger on E and play it three times with an even rhythm.

- **Practice Tip**: Focus on maintaining steady timing and consistent volume across all three E notes.

Phrase 2: E E E

1. **Repeat Phrase 1**: Play E three times with the same rhythm and timing.

- **Practice Tip**: Since this phrase repeats, aim for consistency and accuracy to keep the melody smooth and clear.

Phrase 3: E G C D E

1. **Start on E**: Play E once.
2. **Slide Up to G**: Move your finger up to reach G and play it once.
3. **Slide Down to C**: Move down to C and play it once.
4. **Slide Up to D**: Move up slightly to reach D and play it once.
5. **Return to E**: Slide up to E for the final note of the phrase.

- **Practice Tip**: This phrase has more movement between notes, so practice smooth slides between E, G, C, D, and E to keep the melody flowing.

Phrase 4: F F F F F E E E E D D E D G

1. **Start on F**: Place your finger on F and play it five times with an even rhythm.
2. **Move Down to E**: Slide down to E and play it four times.
3. **Slide Down to D**: Move down to D and play it twice.
4. **Return to E**: Slide up to E and play it once.
5. **Slide Down to D**: Move down to D and play it once.
6. **Finish on G**: Move up to G for the final note of the phrase.

- **Practice Tip**: This phrase has several repeated notes, so focus on keeping each repetition consistent in timing and volume. Ensure smooth transitions between D, E, and G at the end of the phrase.

Practice Tips for "Jingle Bells"

1. **Use a Moderate, Even Tempo**: Set a metronome to around 60-70 BPM to help maintain a steady rhythm. This tempo will give the melody a cheerful, bouncy feel.

2. **Focus on Repeated Notes**: In Phrases 1, 2, and 4, practice keeping each repeated note (like E or F) even in volume and timing for a smooth, rhythmic sound.

3. **Practice Smooth Slides**: Sliding between notes like E, G, and C without lifting your finger will help create a connected sound. Keep your touch light as you move between each note.

4. **Add Dynamics for Expression**: Try playing the first note of each phrase slightly louder, then softening the following notes. This will add a playful quality to the song and give it a festive feel.

5. **Practice Each Phrase Separately**: Begin by practicing each phrase individually to build confidence with timing and transitions. Once you feel comfortable, connect the phrases for a complete performance.

6. **Play with a Joyful, Light Touch**: "Jingle Bells" is a lively, celebratory song, so play with a joyful touch to capture its festive spirit.

Song 2: "Ode to Joy"

"Ode to Joy" is a well-known melody from Beethoven's *Symphony No. 9*. This song has a simple and uplifting melody, making it perfect for practicing smooth slides, timing, and consistent pitch on the Otamatone. Its structured, flowing phrases are great for beginners, helping you gain confidence and control as you play.

Notes and Phrases

- **Phrase 1**: E E F G G F E D
- **Phrase 2**: C C D E E D D
- **Phrase 3**: E E F G G F E D
- **Phrase 4**: C C D E D C C

Fingering Instructions

Each note corresponds to a specific position on the Otamatone slider. Here's where to locate each note and how to transition smoothly between them:

- **C Note**: Near the lower end of the slider, close to the base.
- **D Note**: Slightly above C, requiring a small upward slide.
- **E Note**: Above D, around the lower-middle section of the slider.
- **F Note**: Just above E, slightly below the middle.
- **G Note**: Around the middle of the slider.

Step-by-Step Instructions for Each Phrase

Phrase 1: E E F G G F E D

1. **Start on E**: Place your finger on E and play it twice.
2. **Slide Up to F**: Move up slightly to reach F and play it once.
3. **Slide Up to G**: Move up to reach G and play it twice.
4. **Return to F**: Slide down to F and play it once.
5. **Return to E**: Slide down to E and play it once.
6. **Finish on D**: Slide down to D for the final note.

- **Practice Tip**: This phrase has a rising and falling pattern. Focus on keeping each transition smooth and even, especially between E, F, and G.

Phrase 2: C C D E E D D

1. **Start on C**: Place your finger on C and play it twice.
2. **Slide Up to D**: Move up slightly to reach D and play it once.
3. **Slide Up to E**: Move up to E and play it twice.
4. **Return to D**: Slide down to D and play it twice.

- **Practice Tip**: This phrase ascends and then briefly descends. Keep each note steady and even, focusing on smooth slides from C to E and back.

Phrase 3: E E F G G F E D

1. **Repeat Phrase 1**: Follow the same steps as in Phrase 1.

- **Practice Tip**: Since this phrase is identical to Phrase 1, focus on accuracy and consistency in each slide and timing.

Phrase 4: C C D E D C C

1. **Start on C**: Play C twice, keeping a steady rhythm.
2. **Slide Up to D**: Move up to reach D and play it once.
3. **Slide Up to E**: Move up to E and play it once.
4. **Return to D**: Slide down to D and play it once.
5. **Finish on C**: Slide down to C and play it twice, letting the final note resonate to close the song.

- **Practice Tip**: This phrase brings the melody to a gentle close. Focus on even timing for each note, letting the last C resonate for a confident finish.

Practice Tips for "Ode to Joy"

1. **Play at a Moderate, Steady Tempo**: "Ode to Joy" has a calm, uplifting feel. Set a metronome to around 60 BPM to help keep the rhythm even, allowing the melody to flow smoothly.

2. **Focus on Smooth Slides**: Sliding between notes without lifting your finger will help create a connected, flowing sound. Keep your touch light as you move between notes like E, F, and G.

3. **Maintain Consistent Timing**: Since the song includes repeated notes (such as E and C), make sure each repetition is even in timing and volume. This will keep the melody sounding balanced and smooth.

4. **Add Dynamics for Expression**: Start each phrase softly, then slightly increase the volume as you reach the higher notes,

softening again at the end. This will add warmth and expression to the melody.

5. **Practice Each Phrase Individually**: Start by practicing each phrase on its own until you're comfortable with the transitions and timing. Then, connect the phrases for a smooth, continuous performance.

6. **Play with a Joyful, Light Touch**: "Ode to Joy" is an uplifting song, so try to keep a joyful, flowing touch as you play to capture the song's spirit.

Song 3: "When the Saints Go Marching In"

"When the Saints Go Marching In" is an energetic and upbeat tune, often associated with jazz and gospel music. Its lively melody is perfect for practicing timing, rhythm, and note transitions on the Otamatone. This song provides a great opportunity to work on steady timing and smooth slides between notes.

Notes and Phrases

- **Phrase 1**: C E F G
- **Phrase 2**: C E F G
- **Phrase 3**: G A G F E C E D C
- **Phrase 4**: E E F G C E D C

Fingering Instructions

Each note corresponds to a specific position on the Otamatone slider. Here's where to locate each note and how to transition smoothly between them:

- **C Note**: Near the lower end of the slider, close to the base.
- **D Note**: Slightly above C.
- **E Note**: Above D, around the lower-middle section.
- **F Note**: Just above E.
- **G Note**: Around the middle of the slider.
- **A Note**: Slightly above G.

Step-by-Step Instructions for Each Phrase

Phrase 1: C E F G

1. **Start on C**: Place your finger near the base of the slider and play C once.
2. **Slide Up to E**: Move up to reach E and play it once.
3. **Slide Up to F**: Move slightly up to reach F and play it once.
4. **Slide Up to G**: Move up to G and play it once.

- **Practice Tip**: This phrase has an ascending pattern. Focus on smooth, even slides between each note to keep the melody connected.

Phrase 2: C E F G

1. **Repeat Phrase 1**: Follow the same steps as in Phrase 1.

- **Practice Tip**: Since this phrase repeats, aim for consistency in timing and smoothness as you transition between notes.

Phrase 3: G A G F E C E D C

1. **Start on G**: Place your finger around the middle of the slider and play G once.
2. **Slide Up to A**: Move up slightly to reach A and play it once.
3. **Return to G**: Slide down to G and play it once.
4. **Slide Down to F**: Move down to F and play it once.
5. **Slide Down to E**: Move down to E and play it once.
6. **Return to C**: Slide down to C and play it once.
7. **Slide Up to E**: Move up to reach E and play it once.
8. **Slide Down to D**: Move slightly down to D and play it once.

9. **Finish on C**: Slide down to C for the final note.

- **Practice Tip**: This phrase combines ascending and descending notes. Focus on smooth, precise transitions and maintaining a steady rhythm.

Phrase 4: E E F G C E D C

1. **Start on E**: Place your finger on E and play it twice.
2. **Slide Up to F**: Move slightly up to reach F and play it once.
3. **Slide Up to G**: Move up to G and play it once.
4. **Return to C**: Slide down to C and play it once.
5. **Slide Up to E**: Move up to reach E and play it once.
6. **Slide Down to D**: Move slightly down to D and play it once.

7. **Finish on C**: Slide down to C for the final note.

- **Practice Tip**: Pay attention to the repeated E notes at the beginning, keeping them steady. Smoothly transition through the rest of the phrase, letting the final C ring out.

Practice Tips for "When the Saints Go Marching In"

1. **Set a Moderate, March-Like Tempo**: Since this song has a march-like feel, set a metronome to around 70-80 BPM to help keep a steady rhythm. This will give the song a lively, energetic character.

2. **Focus on Smooth Transitions**: Sliding between notes like C, E, and F without lifting your finger will help maintain a connected, flowing sound. Practice keeping a light, consistent touch as you move between each note.

3. **Work on Repeated Notes**: In Phrase 4, where E repeats, focus on keeping each note even in timing and volume. This will keep the melody sounding steady and rhythmic.

4. **Add Dynamics for Expression**: For added effect, start each phrase with a strong, clear note, then gradually soften as you play through the phrase. This will add a sense of movement and excitement.

5. **Practice Each Phrase Individually**: Begin by practicing each phrase separately to get comfortable with the timing and transitions. Once you feel confident, connect the phrases for a smooth, cohesive performance.

6. **Play with an Energetic Touch**: This song has a celebratory feel, so try to keep a lively, enthusiastic touch as you play to capture the song's upbeat spirit.

Song 4: "London Bridge"

"London Bridge" is a classic children's song with a simple, catchy melody that's easy to learn on the Otamatone. This tune provides an excellent opportunity to practice steady timing, smooth slides, and accurate note transitions, making it a great song for beginners.

Notes and Phrases

- **Phrase 1**: G A G F E F G D
- **Phrase 2**: E F G E F G
- **Phrase 3**: G A G F E F G D
- **Phrase 4**: E G D G

Fingering Instructions

Here's where to locate each note on the Otamatone slider and how to move smoothly between them:

- **D Note**: Slightly above the base of the slider.

- **E Note**: Just above D, closer to the lower-middle section.
- **F Note**: Slightly above E.
- **G Note**: Around the middle of the slider.
- **A Note**: Slightly above G.

Step-by-Step Instructions for Each Phrase

Phrase 1: G A G F E F G D

1. **Start on G**: Place your finger around the middle of the slider and play G once.
2. **Slide Up to A**: Move slightly up to reach A and play it once.
3. **Return to G**: Slide back down to G and play it once.
4. **Slide Down to F**: Move slightly down to F and play it once.
5. **Slide Down to E**: Move down to E and play it once.
6. **Return to F**: Slide up to F and play it once.

7. **Return to G**: Slide back up to G and play it once.

8. **Finish on D**: Slide down to D for the final note.

- **Practice Tip**: This phrase has an ascending and descending pattern. Focus on making each slide smooth and even, especially from G to A and back to G.

Phrase 2: E F G E F G

1. **Start on E**: Place your finger on E and play it once.

2. **Slide Up to F**: Move slightly up to F and play it once.

3. **Slide Up to G**: Move up to G and play it once.

4. **Return to E**: Slide down to E and play it once.

5. **Slide Up to F**: Move up to F again and play it once.

6. **Finish on G**: Slide up to G for the final note of the phrase.

- **Practice Tip**: This phrase moves up and down between E, F, and G. Keep each slide light and connected to create a smooth melody.

Phrase 3: G A G F E F G D

1. **Repeat Phrase 1**: Follow the same steps as in Phrase 1.

- **Practice Tip**: Since this phrase is identical to Phrase 1, aim for consistency in timing and accuracy in each slide.

Phrase 4: E G D G

1. **Start on E**: Place your finger on E and play it once.

2. **Slide Up to G**: Move up to G and play it once.

3. **Return to D**: Slide down to D and play it once.

4. **Finish on G**: Slide back up to G for the final note, allowing it to resonate.

- **Practice Tip**: This phrase has a mix of up-and-down slides. Focus on smooth transitions, especially between D and G, to bring the melody to a gentle close.

Practice Tips for "London Bridge"

1. **Use a Moderate Tempo**: Set a metronome to around 60-70 BPM to help keep each note steady and even. This pace gives the song a cheerful, easy-to-follow rhythm.

2. **Focus on Smooth Slides**: Sliding between notes like G, A, and F without lifting your finger will create a connected sound. Practice keeping your touch light and consistent as you move between each note.

3. **Maintain Consistent Timing**: This song has several repeated patterns, so focus on keeping each note and phrase even in timing and volume to create a steady, flowing melody.

4. **Add Dynamics for Expression**: Start each phrase with a clear, strong note, then soften as you move through the phrase. This will give the song a playful, sing-song quality.

5. **Practice Each Phrase Separately**: Begin by practicing each phrase individually to get comfortable with timing and transitions. Once you feel confident, connect the phrases for a smooth performance.

6. **Play with a Cheerful Touch**: "London Bridge" is a playful song, so try to keep a light, cheerful touch as you play to capture the song's lively spirit.

Song 5. "Twinkle Twinkle Little Star"

"Twinkle Twinkle Little Star" is a simple, well-known melody that's perfect for practicing basic pitch accuracy, smooth transitions, and steady rhythm. This tutorial will guide you through each phrase with detailed finger placement and slider positioning.

Notes and Phrases

- **Phrase 1**: C C G G A A G
- **Phrase 2**: F F E E D D C
- **Phrase 3**: G G F F E E D
- **Phrase 4**: G G F F E E D
- **Phrase 5**: C C G G A A G
- **Phrase 6**: F F E E D D C

Fingering Instructions

Each note requires a specific placement along the Otamatone's slider. Here's a breakdown of the notes, their approximate positions, and how to move smoothly between them.

- **C Note**: Start near the bottom of the slider, closer to the body of the Otamatone. Use your index finger for accuracy.
- **G Note**: Slide up to the middle section of the slider to reach G. This note should be about halfway along the slider.
- **A Note**: Move slightly above G to find A. This is a small shift up from G.
- **F Note**: Located just below G, F is a slight slide down from G.
- **E Note**: Found between F and D, slightly lower than F.
- **D Note**: Place your finger a bit lower than E, moving toward the bottom of the slider.

Step-by-Step Instructions for Each Phrase

Phrase 1: C C G G A A G

1. **Start on C**: Position your finger at the lower part of the slider. Play C twice, holding each note steadily.
2. **Slide to G**: Move your finger up to the middle of the slider to reach G. Play G twice with a light, even pressure.
3. **Move to A**: Slide up slightly from G to A and play it twice.
4. **Return to G**: Slide back down to G for the last note of the phrase.

- **Practice Tip**: Focus on a smooth slide between C and G, and between G and A. These transitions are key to making the melody sound connected.

Phrase 2: F F E E D D C

1. **Start on F**: Position your finger just below G to find F. Play F twice, keeping an even tone.

2. **Slide Down to E**: Move down slightly from F to reach E. Play E twice.

3. **Move to D**: Slide a bit further down the slider to reach D, and play D twice.

4. **Return to C**: Slide down to C for the final note.

- **Practice Tip**: Practice sliding from F to E smoothly to avoid any abrupt pitch changes. Maintaining a steady finger pressure as you slide down to D and C will help make the phrase sound smooth.

Phrase 3: G G F F E E D

1. **Start on G**: Find G at the middle of the slider and play it twice.

2. **Slide Down to F**: Move your finger slightly lower to F and play it twice.

3. **Move to E**: Slide down to E and play it twice.

4. **End on D**: Slide down to D to complete the phrase.

- **Practice Tip**: This phrase mirrors Phrase 2 but with a shorter ending. Focus on making each transition clear, especially the movement between F, E, and D.

Phrase 4: G G F F E E D

- Repeat Phrase 3 exactly as described above. Consistent repetition will help reinforce your finger placement and build muscle memory.

Phrase 5: C C G G A A G

1. Repeat Phrase 1 exactly as described earlier.

Phrase 6: F F E E D D C

1. Repeat Phrase 2 exactly as described earlier. This brings the song to a gentle conclusion on C.

Practice Tips for "Twinkle Twinkle Little Star"

1. **Work in Phrases**: Start by practicing each phrase individually. Play Phrase 1 repeatedly until you're comfortable with the transitions between C, G, and A. Then move on to Phrase 2, and so on.

2. **Slow Down Difficult Transitions**: Pay special attention to any transitions that feel challenging. For example, moving from G to F, or from E to D, may require extra practice to ensure smoothness. Slow down the tempo and focus on consistent pressure and sliding motion.

3. **Use a Metronome**: Set a metronome to a slow tempo, like 60 BPM, to keep each note evenly timed. This will help you play rhythmically and avoid rushing.

4. **Add Dynamics**: Once you're comfortable with the notes, experiment with dynamics. Try playing the beginning phrases softly,

gradually increasing volume with each phrase, then softening again in the final phrase for a gentle ending.

5. **Use Vibrato on the Last Note**: Add a slight vibrato on the final C note by gently pulsing the mouth of the Otamatone. This gives the ending a more expressive touch and adds a sense of closure to the melody.

Song 6. "Mary Had a Little Lamb"

"Mary Had a Little Lamb" is an ideal beginner song for practicing note transitions, rhythm, and pitch accuracy. This simple melody is repetitive and follows a straightforward pattern, making it a perfect choice to build confidence on the Otamatone.

Notes and Phrases

- **Phrase 1**: E D C D E EE
- **Phrase 2**: D DD E G G

- **Phrase 3**: E D C D E EE
- **Phrase 4**: E D D E D C

Fingering Instructions

To help you play each note accurately, here is a breakdown of the approximate slider positions and finger placements for each note in the song:

- **E Note**: Found around the middle of the slider. Use a light touch with your index finger to start.
- **D Note**: Slightly below E, move your finger down a small distance to reach D.
- **C Note**: Located further down the slider, closer to the bottom. This requires a more significant slide down from E.
- **G Note**: Higher up the slider, a little above E. Move up carefully to reach G from E.

Step-by-Step Instructions for Each Phrase

Phrase 1: E D C D E EE

1. **Start on E**: Place your finger at the middle of the slider to play E. Hold it steadily and then release.
2. **Move Down to D**: Slide your finger slightly down the slider to reach D. Hold and release.
3. **Slide to C**: Move further down the slider to reach C and play it once.
4. **Return to D**: Slide back up slightly to D, keeping the movement smooth and steady.
5. **Repeat E**: Slide back up to E and play it three times in a row, aiming for a consistent tone each time.

- **Practice Tip**: Focus on keeping each note even in volume and timing. This phrase has several repeated notes, so concentrate on making each E sound identical for a consistent melody.

Phrase 2: D DD E G G

1. **Start on D**: Place your finger on the slider to find D and play it three times, keeping each D steady and at the same volume.

2. **Move Up to E**: Slide up slightly from D to E, holding this note for a moment to let it resonate.

3. **Slide Up to G**: Move higher on the slider to reach G and play it twice.

- **Practice Tip**: The transition from E to G can be a bit challenging. Practice sliding from E to G slowly and smoothly, making sure to hit each note accurately.

Phrase 3: E D C D E EE

1. **Repeat Phrase 1**: Play the same notes and follow the same steps as in Phrase 1,

focusing on consistent timing and smooth transitions.

- **Practice Tip**: Since this phrase is identical to Phrase 1, use it to reinforce the sliding motions between E, D, and C.

Phrase 4: E D D E D C

1. **Start on E**: Begin with E, located at the middle of the slider.
2. **Move Down to D**: Slide down to D and play it twice.
3. **Return to E**: Slide back up to E and hold it steadily.
4. **Slide to D**: Move slightly down to D, then finish by sliding down to C for the last note of the phrase.

- **Practice Tip**: This phrase has a downward sequence ending on C. Focus on smooth downward slides between E, D, and C to maintain a connected sound as the song concludes.

Practice Tips for "Mary Had a Little Lamb"

1. **Work on Repeated Notes**: Several phrases in this song have repeated notes, particularly E and D. Practice these repeated notes with steady volume and even timing to ensure consistency.

2. **Break Down Each Phrase**: Practice each phrase separately, focusing on accuracy and smooth slides. Once you're comfortable with each phrase individually, connect them to play the full song.

3. **Use a Metronome**: Start with a slow tempo, such as 60 BPM, to ensure you're playing in rhythm. Gradually increase the tempo as you become more comfortable with the timing.

4. **Experiment with Dynamics**: Add some volume variation to create a sense of musical expression. For instance, play the

first phrase softly, then increase the volume on the second phrase to add contrast.

5. **Focus on Smooth Transitions**: "Mary Had a Little Lamb" requires fluid slides between notes, particularly in phrases that move between E, D, and C. Try to avoid abrupt changes by practicing gradual slides and keeping your finger pressure consistent.

Song 7. "Happy Birthday"

"Happy Birthday" is a familiar melody with varied note transitions, making it a great song for practicing timing, pitch accuracy, and expression on the Otamatone. This tune has a distinctive rhythm that is fun to play once you get comfortable with the sliding and finger placement.

Notes and Phrases

- **Phrase 1**: G G A G C B
- **Phrase 2**: G G A G D C

- **Phrase 3**: G GG E C B A
- **Phrase 4**: F F E C D C

Fingering Instructions

Each note corresponds to a specific slider position. Here's a breakdown of how to locate each note and move smoothly between them:

- **G Note**: Found around the middle of the slider. Start with this position as your home base.
- **A Note**: Slightly above G. Slide up carefully to reach A.
- **C Note**: Further down the slider, closer to the bottom.
- **B Note**: Just above C, so only a small movement is needed to reach it.
- **D Note**: Slightly above C, in the middle range.
- **E Note**: Higher up from D, closer to the upper middle of the slider.

123

- **F Note**: Just below G; slide down slightly from G to find F.

Step-by-Step Instructions for Each Phrase

Phrase 1: G G A G C B

1. **Start on G**: Place your finger around the middle of the slider. Play G twice, holding each note steadily.
2. **Move Up to A**: Slide your finger up slightly from G to A and play it once.
3. **Return to G**: Slide back down to G and play it once.
4. **Slide Down to C**: Move your finger down to the lower part of the slider to reach C, and play it once.
5. **Move to B**: Slide up slightly from C to B for the final note of the phrase.

- **Practice Tip**: Focus on the transition between G and A, and then the slide from G down to C. These larger movements will require a steady hand for accuracy.

Phrase 2: G G A G D C

1. **Start on G**: Play G twice, maintaining a consistent tone.
2. **Move Up to A**: Slide up to A and play it once.
3. **Return to G**: Slide back down to G and play it once.
4. **Slide Up to D**: Move your finger up from G to reach D. This will be a slight slide upward.
5. **Move Down to C**: Slide your finger down to C for the final note.

- **Practice Tip**: Practice moving smoothly between G and D to hit the correct pitch each time. Work on a light, even touch to keep transitions clear.

Phrase 3: G GG E C B A

1. **Start on G**: Play G three times, evenly spaced with a steady volume.
2. **Slide Up to E**: Move up from G to reach E. This will require a more significant slide.
3. **Move Down to C**: Slide down to the lower part of the slider to reach C.
4. **Move Up to B**: Slide slightly up from C to reach B.
5. **Slide Down to A**: Move your finger down to A for the final note.

- **Practice Tip**: Focus on the jump from G to E, as this movement may be tricky at first. Go slowly to get used to the distances involved.

Phrase 4: F F E C D C

1. **Start on F**: Find F just below G and play it twice.

126

2. **Slide Up to E**: Move slightly up from F to reach E and play it once.

3. **Move Down to C**: Slide down to the lower part of the slider to reach C and play it once.

4. **Slide Up to D**: Move up slightly from C to reach D and play it once.

5. **Return to C**: Slide back down to C for the final note.

- **Practice Tip**: This phrase has smaller, more controlled movements. Work on hitting each note precisely, especially during the final transition back to C.

Practice Tips for "Happy Birthday"

1. **Work on Rhythm**: "Happy Birthday" has a unique rhythm, especially in the third phrase. Use a metronome or count along to keep the timing consistent, particularly where notes are repeated or held for longer durations.

2. **Phrase-by-Phrase Practice**: Practice each phrase individually before attempting to play the entire song. Once you're comfortable with each part, try combining the phrases to play the full melody.

3. **Focus on Larger Jumps**: Some transitions, like G to E and G to D, involve larger movements. Practice these transitions slowly at first to improve accuracy. A steady slide with consistent pressure will help you land on the correct note each time.

4. **Add Dynamics for Emphasis**: Make the first G of each phrase slightly louder for emphasis, especially in the opening "Happy Birthday" phrase. This adds a sense of phrasing and makes the melody more engaging.

5. **Use Vibrato on Long Notes**: On the last note of each phrase, try adding a gentle vibrato by lightly pulsing the mouth. This

technique adds expression to the song and enhances the ending of each phrase.

Song 8. "Row, Row, Row Your Boat"

"Row, Row, Row Your Boat" is a simple and repetitive song, ideal for beginners working on timing, consistent note accuracy, and smooth transitions. The melody is repetitive and follows a straightforward pattern, making it easy to learn while practicing basic pitch and rhythm control.

Notes and Phrases

- **Phrase 1**: C CC D E
- **Phrase 2**: E D E F G
- **Phrase 3**: C CC G G
- **Phrase 4**: G E E D C

Fingering Instructions

Here's a breakdown of each note's position on the slider and the best way to move smoothly between them.

- **C Note**: Located near the lower part of the slider, closer to the base.
- **D Note**: Slightly above C; requires a small upward slide.
- **E Note**: Above D, about halfway up the slider.
- **F Note**: Slightly above E; requires a small slide up from E.
- **G Note**: Higher up, located a bit above F and closer to the middle of the slider.

Step-by-Step Instructions for Each Phrase

Phrase 1: C CC D E

1. **Start on C**: Place your finger near the bottom of the slider to play C. Play it three

times, maintaining consistent timing and tone.

2. **Slide Up to D**: Move your finger slightly up the slider to reach D. Play it once, keeping the transition smooth.

3. **Slide Up to E**: Move up further to reach E and play it once.

- **Practice Tip**: Practice the transition from C to D and then to E carefully. This phrase has a steady, ascending pattern, so work on sliding smoothly and keeping the timing even.

Phrase 2: E D E F G

1. **Start on E**: Place your finger on the slider at the E position and play it once.

2. **Slide Down to D**: Move your finger slightly down to D and play it once.

3. **Return to E**: Slide back up to E and play it once more.

4. **Slide Up to F**: Move up slightly from E to reach F and play it once.

5. **Slide Up to G**: Move further up from F to reach G and play it once.

- **Practice Tip**: This phrase has a lot of movement up and down between notes. Practice sliding between E and D a few times to develop smooth transitions, then work on reaching F and G without lifting your finger.

Phrase 3: C CC G G

1. **Return to C**: Slide back down to C and play it three times, keeping each note even in timing and volume.

2. **Move Up to G**: Slide your finger up to G, near the middle of the slider, and play it twice.

- **Practice Tip**: The jump from C to G requires a large slide. Practice this transition separately if needed, moving slowly at first and then speeding up as you get more comfortable.

Phrase 4: G E E D C

1. **Start on G**: Begin by playing G and hold it briefly to mark the beginning of the final phrase.
2. **Slide Down to E**: Move your finger down from G to E and play it twice in a row.
3. **Move Down to D**: Slide down slightly from E to reach D and play it once.
4. **Finish on C**: Slide further down to C for the final note of the song.

- **Practice Tip**: This descending pattern from G to C should sound smooth and connected. Focus on maintaining consistent finger pressure on the slider as you move down the notes to avoid any pitch fluctuations.

Practice Tips for "Row, Row, Row Your Boat"

1. **Work Slowly on Transitions**: Since this song involves sliding between each note, practice each transition at a slower pace before attempting to play the full song. Pay special attention to larger jumps, like moving from C to G in Phrase 3.

2. **Keep a Steady Rhythm**: Use a metronome set to a slow tempo, such as 60 BPM, to ensure you're playing in time. Gradually increase the tempo as you become more comfortable with the timing and note transitions.

3. **Repeat Each Phrase Individually**: Practice each phrase multiple times until you feel confident, then connect them to play the entire song. This approach will make it

easier to build muscle memory for each sequence.

4. **Use Dynamics for Expressiveness**: Try playing each phrase with slight variations in volume. For example, start the song softly and gradually increase the volume, then end softly on the final phrase. This adds expressiveness to the melody and makes it more engaging.

5. **Practice Consistency with Repeated Notes**: Since Phrases 1 and 3 contain repeated C notes, focus on making each one sound identical. Aim for a steady tone and volume with each repeated note.

Song 9. "Old MacDonald Had a Farm"

"Old MacDonald Had a Farm" is a fun and engaging melody for beginners, with repeating phrases that make it relatively easy to learn. This song is a great way to practice finger placement,

135

pitch accuracy, and steady rhythm on the Otamatone.

Notes and Phrases

- **Phrase 1**: G GG D E E D
- **Phrase 2**: B BAA G
- **Phrase 3**: D D G GG D E E D
- **Phrase 4**: B BAA G

Fingering Instructions

Here's a guide to locating each note and moving between them smoothly on the slider:

- **G Note**: Around the middle of the slider. Start by finding this note as it serves as the home base for the melody.
- **D Note**: Slightly below G, requiring a small downward slide.
- **E Note**: Above D but below G, closer to the lower middle section of the slider.

- **B Note**: Higher than G, further up on the slider.
- **A Note**: Slightly below B, requiring a small slide down from B.

Step-by-Step Instructions for Each Phrase

Phrase 1: G GG D E E D

1. **Start on G**: Position your finger around the middle of the slider to play G. Play G three times with an even rhythm.
2. **Slide Down to D**: Move your finger slightly down to find D, and play it once.
3. **Move Up to E**: Slide your finger up slightly from D to reach E and play it twice.
4. **Return to D**: Slide back down to D for the last note of the phrase.

- **Practice Tip**: Focus on keeping each G note steady and even, as this repetition sets the melody's rhythm. The movement between D and E should be smooth and connected.

Phrase 2: B BAA G

1. **Start on B**: Slide your finger up to B, found higher up on the slider, and play it twice.
2. **Slide Down to A**: Move slightly down from B to reach A and play it twice.
3. **Return to G**: Slide down further from A to reach G, playing it once to end the phrase.

- **Practice Tip**: Since this phrase includes both B and A, practice sliding between these two notes until you're confident in their positions. These movements require precision to hit each note accurately.

Phrase 3: D D G GG D E E D

1. **Start on D**: Return to D (below G) and play it twice.

2. **Move Up to G**: Slide up to G and play it three times with a steady rhythm.

3. **Slide Down to D**: Return to D and play it once.

4. **Move Up to E**: Slide up from D to reach E and play it twice.

5. **Return to D**: Finish the phrase on D, sliding back down smoothly.

- **Practice Tip**: This phrase combines repetition with varied movements. Focus on making each G note sound consistent, and work on the transition from G to D and back to E with a smooth slide.

Phrase 4: B BAA G

1. **Repeat Phrase 2**: Play the same notes and follow the same steps as in Phrase 2. Practice moving steadily between B, A, and G to maintain a connected sound.

Practice Tips for "Old MacDonald Had a Farm"

1. **Emphasize Repeated Notes**: Both G and D are repeated multiple times throughout the song. Practice keeping these notes consistent in tone, volume, and timing. Repetition with precision will make the melody sound smooth and polished.

2. **Practice Phrases Separately**: Begin by practicing each phrase individually. Once you feel confident with each part, connect them to play the entire song seamlessly.

3. **Use a Metronome**: Set a metronome to a slow tempo, like 60 BPM, to keep a steady rhythm. This will help you maintain even timing, especially with the repeated notes in Phrases 1 and 3.

4. **Dynamic Variation**: Add expression to the melody by playing certain notes or phrases slightly louder or softer. For example, play

the first G in each phrase a bit louder to add emphasis, or make the repeated B and A notes in Phrases 2 and 4 softer for variation.

5. **Focus on Smooth Transitions**: Sliding between notes like B and A, or D and E, requires a smooth and controlled finger motion. Avoid lifting your finger when moving between notes; instead, keep a light, consistent pressure on the slider.

Song 10. "The Itsy Bitsy Spider"

"The Itsy Bitsy Spider" is a familiar nursery rhyme melody that's ideal for beginners. This song provides practice in smooth note transitions, steady rhythm, and dynamics. The repetitive phrases make it easy to memorize and play with confidence on the Otamatone.

Notes and Phrases

- **Phrase 1**: C CC D E

- **Phrase 2**: E D C D E EE
- **Phrase 3**: D DD E G G
- **Phrase 4**: C CC G G

Fingering Instructions

Each note corresponds to a specific slider position. Here's a breakdown of where to place your finger for each note and how to smoothly transition between them.

- **C Note**: Located near the lower end of the slider, close to the base.
- **D Note**: Slightly above C, requiring a small upward slide.
- **E Note**: Above D, about halfway up the slider.
- **G Note**: Higher up on the slider, closer to the middle.

Step-by-Step Instructions for Each Phrase

Phrase 1: C CC D E

1. **Start on C**: Place your finger near the bottom of the slider. Play C three times with consistent timing and tone.
2. **Slide Up to D**: Move your finger slightly up from C to reach D. Play it once, keeping the movement smooth.
3. **Slide Up to E**: Move further up from D to reach E and play it once.

- **Practice Tip**: This phrase has an ascending pattern. Focus on a smooth, continuous slide from C to D to E, making sure each note transition sounds connected.

Phrase 2: E D C D E EE

1. **Start on E**: Place your finger at the E position and play it once.

2. **Slide Down to D**: Move your finger down slightly from E to reach D and play it once.

3. **Slide Down to C**: Continue sliding down to C and play it once.

4. **Return to D**: Slide back up to D and play it once.

5. **Play E Three Times**: Slide up to E again and play it three times to complete the phrase.

- **Practice Tip**: Focus on maintaining consistent timing, especially for the repeated E notes at the end. Work on smooth transitions between E, D, and C for a flowing sound.

Phrase 3: D DD E G G

1. **Start on D**: Position your finger on D and play it three times in a steady rhythm.

2. **Slide Up to E**: Move slightly up from D to reach E and play it once.

144

3. **Move Up to G**: Slide further up to reach G and play it twice to end the phrase.

- **Practice Tip**: Practice the transition from D to E to G, as it requires a smooth upward slide. Repeat this phrase slowly to develop consistency with each note.

Phrase 4: C CC G G

1. **Return to C**: Slide back down to C and play it three times.
2. **Move Up to G**: Slide up to G and play it twice to finish the phrase and the song.

- **Practice Tip**: This phrase has a large slide between C and G. Take it slowly at first, practicing a smooth and controlled slide from the lower end of the slider (C) to the middle (G).

Practice Tips for "The Itsy Bitsy Spider"

1. **Practice Each Phrase Individually**: Start by practicing each phrase on its own. Once you're comfortable with each part, connect them to play the full song. This approach will help you build confidence in playing the whole melody.

2. **Use a Steady Rhythm**: The rhythm of this song is steady and consistent. Use a metronome set at a slow tempo (around 60 BPM) to keep each note evenly timed, especially with repeated notes like C and E.

3. **Focus on Transitions**: Sliding between C, D, and E in the ascending and descending phrases is key to making the song sound smooth. Practice these transitions repeatedly to avoid any choppy or abrupt sounds.

4. **Add Dynamics for Expression**: Try adding dynamics by playing the beginning of each phrase softly and increasing volume on the

last note. This will add an expressive quality to the melody and make it more engaging.

5. **Practice Repeated Notes for Consistency**: Since this song has several repeated notes (e.g., C in Phrase 1 and E in Phrase 2), focus on keeping each repeated note steady and even in tone and volume.

Song 11. "Baa Baa Black Sheep"

"Baa Baa Black Sheep" is a well-loved children's song that is simple yet effective for practicing note transitions and rhythm. This song features repetitive phrases, making it a great choice for beginners who want to build confidence with smooth sliding and consistent timing on the Otamatone.

Notes and Phrases

- **Phrase 1**: G G D D E E D
- **Phrase 2**: C C B B A A G

- **Phrase 3**: D D G GG F E D
- **Phrase 4**: C C B BAA G

Fingering Instructions

Each note corresponds to a specific slider position on the Otamatone. Here's a breakdown of where to place your finger for each note:

- **G Note**: Around the middle of the slider. Use this note as your home base.
- **D Note**: Found slightly below G, requiring a small downward slide.
- **E Note**: Located between D and G, a small slide above D.
- **C Note**: Located further down the slider, closer to the bottom.
- **B Note**: Slightly above C, requiring a small slide up from C.
- **A Note**: Above B, but still below G.
- **F Note**: Just below G.

Step-by-Step Instructions for Each Phrase

Phrase 1: G G D D E E D

1. **Start on G**: Position your finger around the middle of the slider. Play G twice with even timing.

2. **Slide Down to D**: Move your finger down to D and play it twice.

3. **Move Up to E**: Slide up slightly from D to reach E, and play it twice.

4. **Return to D**: Slide back down to D for the last note of the phrase.

- **Practice Tip**: Focus on maintaining an even rhythm with the repeated G and D notes. Practice the transition between D and E for a smooth slide.

Phrase 2: C C B BAA G

1. **Start on C**: Move down the slider to reach C, closer to the bottom. Play C twice.
2. **Slide Up to B**: Move slightly up from C to reach B, and play it twice.
3. **Move Up to A**: Slide up from B to A and play it twice.
4. **Return to G**: Slide up to G for the final note of the phrase.

- **Practice Tip**: Since this phrase involves moving up gradually from C to B and then to A, practice these transitions slowly to improve accuracy.

Phrase 3: D D G GG F E D

1. **Start on D**: Begin by playing D twice with a steady rhythm.

2. **Slide Up to G**: Move your finger up to G and play it three times, keeping each note even in timing.

3. **Slide Down to F**: Move slightly down from G to F and play it once.

4. **Move Down to E**: Slide down further from F to reach E and play it once.

5. **Return to D**: Slide down to D for the last note.

- **Practice Tip**: This phrase combines upward and downward slides. Focus on keeping each repeated G note consistent and practice moving down through F, E, and D for smooth transitions.

Phrase 4: C C B BAA G

1. **Repeat Phrase 2**: Follow the same instructions as in Phrase 2 to complete the song.

Practice Tips for "Baa Baa Black Sheep"

1. **Work on Repeated Notes**: This song has multiple repeated notes, such as G and D in the first phrase. Practice keeping each repeated note steady and consistent in volume to maintain a smooth flow.

2. **Practice Phrases Individually**: Start by practicing each phrase on its own. Once you feel comfortable with each part, connect the phrases to play the entire melody.

3. **Focus on Smooth Transitions**: Sliding between notes like C, B, A, and G requires careful, smooth movements. Practice these transitions slowly to avoid abrupt or choppy sounds.

4. **Use a Steady Rhythm**: This song has a simple rhythm that remains steady throughout. Use a metronome set to a slow tempo (around 60 BPM) to keep timing

even. Once you're confident, you can gradually increase the tempo.

5. **Add Dynamics for Expression**: Try adding a bit of expression by varying the volume. For example, play the first note of each phrase slightly louder and soften the other notes to add interest and emphasis.

Song 12. "Frère Jacques"

"Frère Jacques" is a classic French nursery rhyme with a simple, repetitive melody, making it perfect for beginners on the Otamatone. This song provides a great opportunity to practice smooth transitions, pitch accuracy, and rhythm due to its repetitive structure and recognizable melody.

Notes and Phrases

- **Phrase 1**: C D E C
- **Phrase 2**: C D E C
- **Phrase 3**: E F G

- **Phrase 4**: E F G
- **Phrase 5**: G A G F E C
- **Phrase 6**: G A G F E C

Fingering Instructions

Each note corresponds to a specific position on the Otamatone's slider. Here's how to locate each note and move between them smoothly:

- **C Note**: Found near the bottom of the slider.
- **D Note**: Slightly above C, requiring a small upward slide.
- **E Note**: Higher than D, roughly halfway up the slider.
- **F Note**: Just above E, requiring a slight upward slide.
- **G Note**: Located closer to the middle of the slider.
- **A Note**: Higher up on the slider, slightly above G.

Step-by-Step Instructions for Each Phrase

Phrase 1: C D E C

1. **Start on C**: Place your finger near the bottom of the slider. Play C once.
2. **Slide Up to D**: Move your finger slightly up from C to reach D and play it once.
3. **Move Up to E**: Slide up further to reach E and play it once.
4. **Return to C**: Slide down back to C and play it once.

- **Practice Tip**: Focus on smooth, connected slides between C, D, and E. This phrase repeats, so aim to play it consistently each time.

Phrase 2: C D E C

1. **Repeat Phrase 1**: Follow the exact steps as in Phrase 1.

- **Practice Tip**: Since this phrase is identical to the first, use it to reinforce your muscle memory for sliding smoothly between these three notes.

Phrase 3: E F G

1. **Start on E**: Place your finger on E (located about halfway up the slider) and play it once.
2. **Slide Up to F**: Move slightly up from E to reach F and play it once.
3. **Slide Up to G**: Continue sliding up from F to G and play it once.

- **Practice Tip**: Practice the gradual slide up from E to F and then to G. This phrase involves an ascending pattern, so keep the movement smooth and controlled.

Phrase 4: E F G

1. **Repeat Phrase 3**: Follow the exact steps as in Phrase 3.

- **Practice Tip**: As with Phrase 2, this repetition will help reinforce accuracy and control as you move between E, F, and G.

Phrase 5: G A G F E C

1. **Start on G**: Place your finger on G and play it once.
2. **Slide Up to A**: Move up from G to A and play it once.
3. **Return to G**: Slide back down to G and play it once.
4. **Slide Down to F**: Move down to F and play it once.
5. **Continue to E**: Slide further down to E and play it once.

6. **Finish on C**: Slide all the way down to C for the final note of the phrase.

- **Practice Tip**: This phrase involves both ascending and descending movements. Pay attention to smooth transitions, especially when sliding back down from A to G, and then continuing down to F, E, and C.

Phrase 6: G A G F E C

1. **Repeat Phrase 5**: Follow the exact steps as in Phrase 5.

- **Practice Tip**: Use this repetition to solidify your control over the up-and-down sliding motions. Focus on a steady rhythm to keep the melody flowing naturally.

Practice Tips for "Frère Jacques"

1. **Practice Each Phrase Individually**: Start by practicing each phrase on its own. Once

you're comfortable, connect them in sequence to play the entire song.

2. **Keep a Steady Rhythm**: Use a metronome set to a slow tempo, such as 60 BPM, to maintain a steady beat. Gradually increase the tempo as you feel more comfortable with the timing.

3. **Focus on Smooth Transitions**: Sliding smoothly between notes, especially in phrases with ascending and descending patterns, is essential for making the melody sound connected. Work on maintaining even finger pressure on the slider as you move up and down.

4. **Add Dynamics**: To add expression, try varying the volume slightly. Play the first note of each phrase with a bit more emphasis, then soften the following notes. This creates a sense of phrasing and makes the melody more engaging.

5. **Reinforce Repetition for Consistency**:
Since "Frère Jacques" has repeating phrases, use these repetitions to build consistency in your note accuracy and timing. Practice each phrase until it feels smooth and natural.

Song 13. "Hot Cross Buns"

"Hot Cross Buns" is a simple and repetitive melody that is perfect for beginners. This song uses only three notes and follows a consistent pattern, making it an ideal choice for practicing pitch accuracy, rhythm, and smooth transitions on the Otamatone.

Notes and Phrases

- **Phrase 1**: E D C
- **Phrase 2**: E D C
- **Phrase 3**: C CCC - D DDD - E D C

Fingering Instructions

Each note corresponds to a specific position on the slider. Here's how to find each note and transition smoothly between them:

- **E Note**: Located around the middle of the slider. This is the highest note used in this song.
- **D Note**: Slightly below E, requiring a small downward slide.
- **C Note**: Lower down on the slider, closer to the base of the instrument.

Step-by-Step Instructions for Each Phrase

Phrase 1: E D C

1. **Start on E**: Place your finger around the middle of the slider to play E. Hold it steadily and then release.
2. **Slide Down to D**: Move your finger slightly down from E to reach D and play it once.

161

3. **Slide Down to C**: Continue sliding down to C and play it once.

• **Practice Tip**: Focus on making smooth, connected slides between E, D, and C. This phrase will repeat multiple times, so aim for consistency with each note.

Phrase 2: E D C

1. **Repeat Phrase 1**: Follow the same steps as in Phrase 1.

• **Practice Tip**: Since this phrase is identical to the first, use this repetition to build confidence in your sliding technique and note accuracy.

Phrase 3: C CCC - D DDD - E D C

1. **Start on C**: Play C four times with even timing and volume.

2. **Move Up to D**: Slide up slightly from C to D and play it four times with consistent rhythm.

3. **Move Up to E**: Slide up to E, play it once, then continue with a downward slide.

4. **Slide Down to D and C**: After playing E, slide down to D, play it once, and finish by sliding down to C for the final note.

- **Practice Tip**: This phrase has repeated notes in a simple rhythmic pattern. Focus on keeping each repeated note consistent in volume and timing. Work on the slide from E down to D and C to ensure a smooth, connected ending.

Practice Tips for "Hot Cross Buns"

1. **Work on Consistent Repetitions**: Each phrase has repeated notes, so focus on keeping each note steady in timing and

volume. This consistency will make the melody sound polished and rhythmic.

2. **Practice Smooth Transitions**: Since this song primarily moves between E, D, and C, practice these transitions slowly at first. Keep your finger pressure even and avoid lifting your finger as you slide to maintain a connected sound.

3. **Use a Metronome**: Set a metronome to a slow tempo, like 60 BPM, to keep each note evenly timed. Gradually increase the speed as you become more comfortable with the rhythm and transitions.

4. **Add Dynamics**: Experiment with dynamics by playing certain phrases slightly louder or softer. For example, you can play the repeated C notes softly, then add a little more volume when you move up to D. This will add expressiveness to the melody.

5. **Focus on Finger Positioning**: "Hot Cross Buns" is a simple melody but requires

accurate finger positioning to play each note precisely. Take your time to find E, D, and C on the slider and practice returning to these positions confidently.

Song 14. "Yankee Doodle"

"Yankee Doodle" is a lively and rhythmic American folk song that is great for beginners practicing timing, note accuracy, and transitions on the Otamatone. This song includes both ascending and descending note patterns, which will help you develop control and confidence in sliding smoothly between notes.

Notes and Phrases

- **Phrase 1**: C C D E C E D
- **Phrase 2**: C C D E C B C
- **Phrase 3**: E E F G E G F
- **Phrase 4**: E D E C D C

Fingering Instructions

Here is where to locate each note on the Otamatone's slider:

- **C Note**: Found near the lower end of the slider, closer to the base.
- **D Note**: Slightly above C, requiring a small upward slide.
- **E Note**: Higher up from D, around the middle of the slider.
- **F Note**: Just above E, requiring a slight upward slide.
- **G Note**: Located higher up, above F and closer to the middle-top of the slider.

Step-by-Step Instructions for Each Phrase

Phrase 1: C C D E C E D

1. **Start on C**: Place your finger near the bottom of the slider to play C. Play it twice with even timing.

2. **Slide Up to D**: Move your finger slightly up from C to reach D and play it once.

3. **Slide Up to E**: Move further up to E and play it once.

4. **Return to C**: Slide back down to C and play it once.

5. **Return to E**: Slide up to E and play it once more.

6. **Slide Down to D**: Move your finger down to D for the final note.

- **Practice Tip**: Work on a smooth, controlled slide from C to E and back down to D. These transitions help with rhythm and pitch consistency.

Phrase 2: C C D E C B C

1. **Start on C**: Begin by playing C twice with even timing.

2. **Slide Up to D**: Move slightly up to D and play it once.

3. **Move Up to E**: Slide further up to reach E and play it once.

4. **Return to C**: Slide back down to C and play it once.

5. **Slide Down to B**: Move down slightly from C to reach B and play it once.

6. **Return to C**: Finish by sliding back to C.

- **Practice Tip**: This phrase involves moving up to E and back down to C and B. Practice moving smoothly between these notes for better control over pitch.

Phrase 3: E E F G E G F

1. **Start on E**: Place your finger on E around the middle of the slider and play it twice.

2. **Slide Up to F**: Move slightly up from E to reach F and play it once.

3. **Slide Up to G**: Move further up from F to reach G and play it once.

168

4. **Return to E**: Slide back down to E and play it once.

5. **Return to G**: Slide up to G again and play it once.

6. **Slide Down to F**: Move down to F for the final note.

- **Practice Tip**: This phrase has a lot of back-and-forth movement between E, F, and G. Practice these transitions slowly to build accuracy.

Phrase 4: E D E C D C

1. **Start on E**: Begin by playing E once.

2. **Slide Down to D**: Move slightly down from E to reach D and play it once.

3. **Return to E**: Slide back up to E and play it once more.

4. **Move Down to C**: Slide down further to reach C and play it once.

5. **Return to D**: Slide up slightly to D and play it once.

6. **Finish on C**: Return to C to end the phrase.

- **Practice Tip**: This descending and ascending pattern requires smooth, connected movements. Work on a light, controlled slide between each note for a fluid sound.

Practice Tips for "Yankee Doodle"

1. **Practice Each Phrase Separately**: Break down the song into each phrase and practice them individually before connecting the phrases to play the entire song.

2. **Focus on Consistent Timing**: Use a metronome set to a slow tempo, like 60 BPM, to keep each note steady and even. Gradually increase the tempo as you become more comfortable with the timing.

3. **Smooth Transitions**: Practice sliding between notes like C, D, E, and F without lifting your finger. Keep the motion smooth and light to ensure a connected sound between each note.

4. **Add Dynamics for Expression**: Try adding dynamics by emphasizing certain notes. For example, make the first C of each phrase slightly louder for emphasis, then soften the other notes. This creates a more engaging melody.

5. **Repeat for Consistency**: Since some notes, like C and E, repeat frequently in this song, focus on making each repetition sound consistent in tone and timing.

Song 15. "Silent Night"

"Silent Night" is a beautiful, slow-paced Christmas carol that's perfect for practicing smooth slides, expressive dynamics, and tone control on the Otamatone. This song's gentle melody and flowing rhythm provide an opportunity to focus on creating a warm, connected sound.

Notes and Phrases

- **Phrase 1**: G A G E
- **Phrase 2**: G A G E
- **Phrase 3**: D D E G
- **Phrase 4**: A A G F D
- **Phrase 5**: G A G E
- **Phrase 6**: G A G E
- **Phrase 7**: D D E G
- **Phrase 8**: A A G F D

Fingering Instructions

Here is the placement of each note on the Otamatone slider and guidance on finger movements:

- **G Note**: Around the middle of the slider.
- **A Note**: Slightly above G, requiring a gentle slide up.

172

- **E Note**: Found a bit below G, requiring a downward slide.
- **D Note**: Below E, closer to the lower part of the slider.
- **F Note**: Just below G, slightly higher than E.

Step-by-Step Instructions for Each Phrase

Phrase 1: G A G E

1. **Start on G**: Place your finger around the middle of the slider to play G, holding it briefly.
2. **Slide Up to A**: Move slightly up from G to reach A and play it once.
3. **Return to G**: Slide back down to G for a gentle return.
4. **Slide Down to E**: Move your finger down to E and play it to complete the phrase.

- **Practice Tip**: Focus on a smooth, connected slide between each note. This phrase should feel calm and flowing to match the gentle nature of the song.

Phrase 2: G A G E

1. **Repeat Phrase 1**: Follow the same steps as in Phrase 1.

- **Practice Tip**: Use this repetition to focus on consistent tone and even timing. Aim for a soft, warm sound.

Phrase 3: D D E G

1. **Start on D**: Place your finger below E on the slider and play D twice with steady timing.
2. **Slide Up to E**: Move your finger up to E and play it once.
3. **Slide Up to G**: Continue sliding up from E to reach G and play it once.

- **Practice Tip**: This phrase has a slow, rising feel. Focus on creating a smooth connection between D, E, and G for a gentle, expressive sound.

Phrase 4: A A G F D

1. **Start on A**: Move your finger to A, just above G, and play it twice.
2. **Slide Down to G**: Move your finger down to G and play it once.
3. **Move Down to F**: Slide down slightly from G to reach F and play it once.
4. **Finish on D**: Slide down further to D for the final note.

- **Practice Tip**: Work on keeping the notes connected with a soft touch. The transition from A down to D should sound smooth and flowing.

Phrase 5: G A G E

1. **Repeat Phrase 1**: Follow the same steps as in Phrase 1.

-   **Practice Tip**: This repetition allows you to reinforce the sliding motions between G, A, and E.

Phrase 6: G A G E

1. **Repeat Phrase 1 again**: Follow the same steps as in Phrase 1.

-   **Practice Tip**: Focus on gentle dynamics and even timing, as the song's soft character requires a delicate touch.

Phrase 7: D D E G

1. **Repeat Phrase 3**: Follow the same steps as in Phrase 3.

-   **Practice Tip**: Continue working on smooth, connected movements between D, E, and G.

Phrase 8: A A G F D

1. **Repeat Phrase 4**: Follow the same steps as in Phrase 4.

- **Practice Tip**: This phrase closes the song, so try adding a gentle diminuendo (softening of volume) as you slide down to the final note, D, for a soft, peaceful ending.

Practice Tips for "Silent Night"

1. **Slow, Consistent Tempo**: "Silent Night" is a slow song, so take your time with each note. Use a metronome set to a slow tempo, such as 50 BPM, to ensure each note holds steady without rushing.

2. **Smooth Transitions**: Practice sliding between notes like G, A, and E without lifting your finger. Keep your touch light and controlled to maintain a connected sound between each note.

3. **Focus on Dynamics**: Use dynamics to add expression. Start each phrase softly, increase volume slightly on the middle notes, then return to a softer tone at the end. This will give the song an expressive, warm character.

4. **Repeat Each Phrase for Consistency**: Since "Silent Night" has repetitive phrases, focus on making each repetition sound consistent. Practice each phrase several times until you're comfortable with the transitions and note placements.

5. **Use Vibrato on Long Notes**: For added expression, consider adding a gentle vibrato to longer notes, like the final D in each phrase. Lightly pulse the Otamatone's "mouth" to create a subtle vibrato effect, enhancing the song's emotional quality.

Song 16. "Amazing Grace"

"Amazing Grace" is a beautiful and soulful melody that is ideal for practicing expressive dynamics, smooth transitions, and precise pitch control on the Otamatone. Its slow tempo and flowing notes provide a great opportunity to focus on creating an emotional, connected sound.

Notes and Phrases

- **Phrase 1**: G B D G
- **Phrase 2**: B A G E
- **Phrase 3**: G B D G
- **Phrase 4**: B D B G
- **Phrase 5**: D E G B
- **Phrase 6**: G E D

Fingering Instructions

Here is the approximate slider position for each note, along with tips for smooth transitions:

- **G Note**: Around the middle of the slider. This note is the starting point and will be used often.
- **B Note**: Higher up the slider, above G.
- **D Note**: Located just below G, requiring a gentle downward slide.
- **E Note**: Found just below D, slightly toward the lower end of the slider.
- **A Note**: Between G and B, above G but below B.

Step-by-Step Instructions for Each Phrase

Phrase 1: G B D G

1. **Start on G**: Place your finger around the middle of the slider and play G once.
2. **Slide Up to B**: Move your finger up to B and play it once with a steady tone.
3. **Slide Down to D**: Move your finger down to D, just below G, and play it once.

4. **Return to G**: Slide back up to G for the final note of the phrase.

- **Practice Tip**: Focus on smooth, controlled slides between G, B, and D. This phrase sets the tone for the song, so try to play it with an expressive, gentle touch.

Phrase 2: B A G E

1. **Start on B**: Play B once, allowing the note to resonate.
2. **Slide Down to A**: Move your finger slightly down to reach A and play it once.
3. **Slide Down to G**: Continue sliding down to G and play it once.
4. **Slide Down to E**: Move further down to reach E for the final note.

- **Practice Tip**: This phrase has a descending pattern, so work on keeping each slide smooth and even. Aim for a warm, flowing sound between each note.

Phrase 3: G B D G

1. **Repeat Phrase 1**: Follow the same instructions as in Phrase 1.

- **Practice Tip**: Use this repetition to reinforce smooth, connected transitions between G, B, and D. Try to make each note sound consistent with the first time you played this phrase.

Phrase 4: B D B G

1. **Start on B**: Slide up to B and play it once.
2. **Slide Down to D**: Move your finger down to reach D and play it once.
3. **Return to B**: Slide back up to B and play it again.
4. **Slide Down to G**: Move down to G for the final note.

- **Practice Tip**: This phrase has a back-and-forth motion between B and D. Practice moving smoothly between these two notes to maintain a steady flow.

Phrase 5: D E G B

1. **Start on D**: Begin by playing D with a calm, steady tone.
2. **Slide Down to E**: Move your finger slightly down to reach E and play it once.
3. **Slide Up to G**: Move your finger up to G and play it once.
4. **Move Up to B**: Slide further up from G to reach B and play it once.

- **Practice Tip**: Focus on smooth ascending slides from E to G and then up to B. This phrase has an uplifting feel, so aim for a gentle crescendo as you move up.

Phrase 6: G E D

1. **Start on G**: Position your finger on G and play it once.

2. **Slide Down to E**: Move slightly down to reach E and play it once.

3. **Finish on D**: Slide down to D for the final note, letting it resonate softly.

- **Practice Tip**: This phrase serves as a soft, gentle ending to the song. Try to make each note sound connected and gradually soften your volume as you play the final D for a peaceful finish.

Practice Tips for "Amazing Grace"

1. **Use Slow, Controlled Movements**: "Amazing Grace" is a slow, flowing melody, so take your time with each note. Use a metronome set to a slow tempo (about 50-60 BPM) to help you play in a relaxed, steady rhythm.

2. **Focus on Dynamics**: This song benefits from expressive dynamics. Start each phrase softly, build slightly in the middle notes, and soften again at the end. This will add emotional depth to the melody.

3. **Practice Each Phrase Individually**: Practice each phrase on its own, focusing on smooth transitions and accurate pitch. Once you're comfortable with each phrase, try connecting them to play the entire song.

4. **Work on Smooth Transitions**: Pay special attention to sliding between notes like B and D, or D and G. These transitions should sound connected and natural, so keep your finger pressure light as you move between notes.

5. **Add Gentle Vibrato on Long Notes**: Adding a gentle vibrato to longer notes, such as B or G, can enhance the song's expressive quality. Try lightly pulsing the

Otamatone's "mouth" to create a subtle vibrato effect on these notes.

6. **Play with Feeling**: "Amazing Grace" is an emotional, reflective song. Play it slowly and focus on creating a warm, resonant sound to capture the song's soothing character.

Song 17. "This Little Light of Mine"

"This Little Light of Mine" is an uplifting and rhythmic gospel song that's excellent for practicing timing, consistent pitch, and expressive dynamics on the Otamatone. The repetitive phrases make it easier to learn and provide a great way to work on rhythmic accuracy.

Notes and Phrases

- **Phrase 1**: G G C CC D E
- **Phrase 2**: E D C D E G G
- **Phrase 3**: G G C CC D E

- **Phrase 4**: E D C D G

Fingering Instructions

Each note on the Otamatone corresponds to a different slider position. Here's how to find each note and move between them smoothly:

- **G Note**: Around the middle of the slider.
- **C Note**: Lower down on the slider, closer to the base.
- **D Note**: Slightly above C, requiring a small upward slide.
- **E Note**: Above D, located a bit lower than G.

Step-by-Step Instructions for Each Phrase

Phrase 1: G G C CC D E

1. **Start on G**: Place your finger around the middle of the slider and play G twice with a strong, steady tone.

187

2. **Slide Down to C**: Move your finger down to C and play it three times with a rhythmic pulse.

3. **Slide Up to D**: Move slightly up from C to reach D and play it once.

4. **Slide Up to E**: Move further up to E and play it once.

• **Practice Tip**: Focus on keeping a rhythmic feel, especially with the repeated C notes. Try to play with a steady, pulsing beat to capture the uplifting nature of the song.

Phrase 2: E D C D E G G

1. **Start on E**: Play E once with a strong tone.

2. **Slide Down to D**: Move slightly down from E to D and play it once.

3. **Slide Down to C**: Continue sliding down to C and play it once.

4. **Return to D**: Slide up to D and play it once more.

5. **Move Up to E**: Slide up to E and play it once.

6. **Return to G**: Slide up to G and play it twice to complete the phrase.

- **Practice Tip**: This phrase has an ascending and descending pattern. Work on making each transition smooth and even, especially as you move up and down between C, D, and E.

Phrase 3: G G C CC D E

1. **Repeat Phrase 1**: Follow the same steps as in Phrase 1.

- **Practice Tip**: Since this phrase is identical to the first, use it to reinforce your rhythm and consistency, especially on the repeated C notes.

Phrase 4: E D C D G

1. **Start on E**: Play E once.

2. **Slide Down to D**: Move your finger down slightly to reach D and play it once.

3. **Move Down to C**: Slide down to C and play it once.

4. **Return to D**: Slide up to D and play it once more.

5. **Finish on G**: Slide up to G for the final note, letting it resonate.

- **Practice Tip**: This phrase brings the song to a close. Focus on a steady rhythm and try to end with a strong, resonant G.

Practice Tips for "This Little Light of Mine"

1. **Emphasize the Rhythm**: This song has a lively, rhythmic beat. Use a metronome set to a moderate tempo (around 70 BPM) to keep your timing consistent. Let each note feel energetic and lively to capture the song's joyful spirit.

2. **Focus on Repeated Notes**: There are several repeated notes, especially with C. Practice keeping each repeated note even in timing, volume, and tone to create a steady rhythmic pulse.

3. **Practice Each Phrase Separately**: Break the song down into phrases and practice each one individually. Once you're comfortable, connect the phrases to play the entire song.

4. **Add Dynamics**: Try adding dynamics for expressiveness. For example, start each phrase softly and increase volume as you reach the last few notes. This adds energy to the melody and highlights key parts of the song.

5. **Smooth Transitions**: Focus on smooth sliding transitions, especially between C, D, and E. Avoid lifting your finger when moving between these notes to maintain a connected, flowing sound.

6. **Use Vibrato on Long Notes**: For added expressiveness, consider adding a gentle vibrato on longer notes, like the final G in each phrase. Lightly pulse the "mouth" of the Otamatone to create a subtle vibrato effect that enhances the joyful tone.

Song 18. "Kumbaya"

"Kumbaya" is a beautiful and meditative folk song, perfect for practicing smooth transitions, expressive dynamics, and timing on the Otamatone. Its slow tempo and gentle melody make it ideal for focusing on creating a warm, connected sound.

Notes and Phrases

- **Phrase 1**: G A C C
- **Phrase 2**: D E G G
- **Phrase 3**: A G E D C
- **Phrase 4**: D E G

Fingering Instructions

Here's a guide to locating each note on the slider and moving between them smoothly:

- **G Note**: Around the middle of the slider.
- **A Note**: Slightly above G, requiring a small slide up.
- **C Note**: Found closer to the lower part of the slider.
- **D Note**: Just above C, requiring a slight upward slide.
- **E Note**: Above D, about halfway up the slider.

Step-by-Step Instructions for Each Phrase

Phrase 1: G A C C

1. **Start on G**: Position your finger around the middle of the slider and play G once.
2. **Slide Up to A**: Move slightly up from G to reach A and play it once.

3. **Slide Down to C**: Move your finger down to reach C and play it twice.

- **Practice Tip**: This phrase has a calm, descending feel. Focus on keeping each slide smooth and even, especially the transition from A to C.

Phrase 2: D E G G

1. **Start on D**: Move your finger to D, which is just above C, and play it once.
2. **Slide Up to E**: Move up slightly to reach E and play it once.
3. **Slide Up to G**: Move up to G and play it twice with a soft, steady tone.

- **Practice Tip**: This phrase has an ascending pattern, so work on making each slide upward feel controlled and connected. Let the two G notes resonate slightly to add warmth.

Phrase 3: A G E D C

1. **Start on A**: Place your finger on A and play it once.

2. **Slide Down to G**: Move down from A to reach G and play it once.

3. **Slide Down to E**: Move further down to reach E and play it once.

4. **Slide Down to D**: Continue sliding down to reach D and play it once.

5. **Finish on C**: Slide down to C for the last note in the phrase.

- **Practice Tip**: This phrase has a descending pattern, so focus on smooth downward slides, letting each note flow naturally into the next.

Phrase 4: D E G

1. **Start on D**: Play D once with a gentle, steady tone.

2. **Slide Up to E**: Move slightly up to reach E and play it once.

3. **Finish on G**: Slide up to G for the final note, allowing it to resonate softly to complete the song.

- **Practice Tip**: This final phrase serves as a gentle ending. Focus on an expressive slide up to G, adding a slight diminuendo (softening of volume) for a peaceful finish.

Practice Tips for "Kumbaya"

1. **Slow, Consistent Tempo**: "Kumbaya" is a slow and meditative song, so use a metronome set to a slow tempo (around 50 BPM) to help you keep each note steady and calm. This tempo allows you to focus on the connected sound of each note.

2. **Focus on Smooth Transitions**: Since the melody is flowing, practice sliding between each note without lifting your finger. This

will create a smooth, connected sound, especially in the descending phrases.

3. **Add Dynamics for Expressiveness**: Use dynamics to add expression. Start each phrase softly, increase the volume slightly in the middle, and soften again as you reach the end. This adds an emotional depth to the melody.

4. **Repeat Each Phrase for Consistency**: Practice each phrase several times to build confidence with the transitions and note positions. This will help you play the entire song with a steady, consistent sound.

5. **Use Gentle Vibrato on Long Notes**: On notes like the final G in each phrase, consider adding a gentle vibrato. Lightly pulse the Otamatone's "mouth" to create a subtle vibrato effect that enhances the song's calming tone.

6. **Play with Feeling**: "Kumbaya" has a peaceful, reflective quality. Take your time

with each note and focus on creating a warm, resonant sound to capture the song's soothing character.

Song 19. "My Bonnie Lies Over the Ocean"

"My Bonnie Lies Over the Ocean" is a lively, melodic folk song that is great for practicing pitch accuracy, smooth transitions, and rhythm on the Otamatone. This song has a familiar melody with repeating phrases, which makes it approachable and fun for beginners.

Notes and Phrases

- **Phrase 1**: G C C D E
- **Phrase 2**: G A B C
- **Phrase 3**: C C D E F E D
- **Phrase 4**: E D C D C

Fingering Instructions

Each note corresponds to a specific position on the Otamatone's slider. Here's how to locate each note and transition smoothly between them:

- **G Note**: Around the middle of the slider.
- **A Note**: Slightly above G, requiring a gentle upward slide.
- **B Note**: Above A, closer to the top-middle of the slider.
- **C Note**: Lower down on the slider, closer to the base.
- **D Note**: Just above C, requiring a small upward slide.
- **E Note**: Above D, between D and G.
- **F Note**: Slightly above E, closer to G.

Step-by-Step Instructions for Each Phrase

Phrase 1: G C C D E

1. **Start on G**: Place your finger around the middle of the slider and play G once.
2. **Slide Down to C**: Move your finger down to reach C and play it twice with even timing.
3. **Slide Up to D**: Move slightly up from C to reach D and play it once.
4. **Slide Up to E**: Move up further from D to reach E and play it once to complete the phrase.

- **Practice Tip**: Focus on the transition from C to D and then to E. Practice keeping your slides smooth and consistent in rhythm.

Phrase 2: G A B C

1. **Start on G**: Position your finger on G and play it once.

2. **Slide Up to A**: Move slightly up to reach A and play it once.

3. **Move Up to B**: Slide further up to B and play it once.

4. **Slide Down to C**: Move your finger down to reach C and play it once to end the phrase.

- **Practice Tip**: This phrase has an ascending pattern. Focus on moving smoothly between G, A, and B before sliding down to C.

Phrase 3: C C D E F E D

1. **Start on C**: Play C twice with steady timing.

2. **Slide Up to D**: Move up to D and play it once.

3. **Slide Up to E**: Continue sliding up from D to E and play it once.

4. **Slide Up to F**: Move slightly up from E to reach F and play it once.

5. **Return to E**: Slide back down to E and play it once.

6. **Slide Down to D**: Move down from E to D and play it once to finish the phrase.

- **Practice Tip**: This phrase has a mix of ascending and descending notes. Work on keeping each slide smooth, particularly between E, F, and back down to D.

Phrase 4: E D C D C

1. **Start on E**: Place your finger on E and play it once.

2. **Slide Down to D**: Move your finger down slightly to reach D and play it once.

3. **Slide Down to C**: Move down further to C and play it once.

4. **Return to D**: Slide up to D and play it once.

5. **Finish on C**: Slide back down to C for the final note, letting it resonate to complete the song.

202

- **Practice Tip**: This phrase brings the melody to a close. Focus on a smooth descending slide from E down to C, and add a bit of emphasis to the final note for a strong finish.

Practice Tips for "My Bonnie Lies Over the Ocean"

1. **Emphasize the Rhythm**: This song has a bouncy, rhythmic feel. Use a metronome set to a moderate tempo (around 70 BPM) to help you keep each note steady and consistent.

2. **Work on Repeated Notes**: In phrases with repeated notes like C, make sure each note sounds even and rhythmic. This consistency will help the melody flow naturally.

3. **Practice Each Phrase Individually**: Break down the song into phrases and practice each one separately. Once you're comfortable, connect them to play the entire melody smoothly.

4. **Focus on Smooth Transitions**: Sliding between notes like C, D, and E should feel connected. Avoid lifting your finger; instead, keep a light, controlled pressure on the slider.

5. **Use Dynamics for Expression**: Add dynamics to create a more engaging melody. Try starting each phrase softly, building volume in the middle, and softening at the end. This will give the song an expressive, musical quality.

6. **Add Vibrato on Long Notes**: For an extra touch, add a gentle vibrato on longer notes, such as the final C in each phrase. Lightly pulsing the Otamatone's "mouth" can create a subtle vibrato effect that adds warmth and emotion to the melody.

Song 20. "She'll Be Coming 'Round the Mountain"

"She'll Be Coming 'Round the Mountain" is an upbeat folk song with a catchy and repetitive melody. This song is ideal for practicing rhythmic consistency, smooth transitions, and expressive dynamics on the Otamatone. Its energetic pace provides a fun way to work on timing and note accuracy.

Notes and Phrases

- **Phrase 1**: G G E G A A G
- **Phrase 2**: G G E G A A G
- **Phrase 3**: B B A G A F E
- **Phrase 4**: G G E G A A G

Fingering Instructions

Here's a guide to locating each note on the slider and moving smoothly between them:

- **G Note**: Located around the middle of the slider.
- **E Note**: Below G, slightly toward the lower-middle section.
- **A Note**: Slightly above G, requiring a small upward slide.
- **B Note**: Higher up on the slider, above A.
- **F Note**: Just below G, slightly above E.

Step-by-Step Instructions for Each Phrase

Phrase 1: G G E G A A G

1. **Start on G**: Place your finger around the middle of the slider and play G twice, keeping a steady rhythm.
2. **Slide Down to E**: Move your finger down to reach E and play it once.
3. **Return to G**: Slide up to G and play it once.
4. **Slide Up to A**: Move up slightly from G to reach A and play it twice.

206

5. **Return to G**: Slide back down to G for the final note of the phrase.

- **Practice Tip**: This phrase requires smooth movement between G, E, and A. Keep each slide controlled and focus on a consistent rhythm to capture the lively feel of the song.

Phrase 2: G G E G A A G

1. **Repeat Phrase 1**: Follow the same steps as in Phrase 1.

- **Practice Tip**: Since this phrase is identical to the first, use it to reinforce your rhythm and accuracy on repeated notes. Try adding a bit more emphasis to give the melody energy.

Phrase 3: B B A G A F E

1. **Start on B**: Slide up to B, near the top-middle of the slider, and play it twice.

2. **Slide Down to A**: Move slightly down from B to reach A and play it once.

3. **Slide Down to G**: Move further down to G and play it once.

4. **Return to A**: Slide up to A and play it once more.

5. **Slide Down to F**: Move down to F and play it once.

6. **Finish on E**: Slide down to E for the last note in the phrase.

- **Practice Tip**: This phrase has a mix of descending and ascending notes. Work on smooth transitions between B, A, and G. Let each note feel connected and rhythmic.

Phrase 4: G G E G A A G

1. **Repeat Phrase 1 again**: Follow the same steps as in Phrase 1.

- **Practice Tip**: This final phrase repeats the initial melody, so aim for consistency and finish with a strong, resonant G.

Practice Tips for "She'll Be Coming 'Round the Mountain"

1. **Use a Steady Rhythm**: This song has a lively tempo. Use a metronome set to a moderate tempo (around 80 BPM) to help keep each note even and steady. The rhythm should feel upbeat and energetic, so let the tempo drive your timing.

2. **Work on Consistent Repetitions**: Since many phrases repeat, focus on making each repetition sound identical. Practice the transitions between G, E, and A, as they appear frequently in the melody.

3. **Smooth Transitions**: Sliding between G, A, and E without lifting your finger helps maintain a smooth, connected sound. Keep a

light, controlled touch on the slider to avoid any abrupt changes in pitch.

4. **Add Dynamics for Expression**: Use dynamics to give the song extra character. Start each phrase with a strong, clear G, then vary the volume slightly as you move between notes. This will help make the melody sound more engaging and expressive.

5. **Practice Each Phrase Separately**: Break down the song into phrases and practice each one individually before connecting them. This approach will help you feel more confident when playing the entire melody.

6. **Use Gentle Vibrato on Long Notes**: For added expression, add a slight vibrato on longer notes like the final G in each phrase. Lightly pulse the "mouth" of the Otamatone for a subtle vibrato effect, giving the song a fun, lively twist.

Song 21. "Lavender's Blue"

"Lavender's Blue" is a gentle and melodic folk song that's perfect for practicing smooth transitions, expressive dynamics, and steady timing on the Otamatone. The song's flowing and repetitive nature makes it an ideal choice for beginners who want to focus on creating a warm, connected sound.

Notes and Phrases

- **Phrase 1**: C D E E D C
- **Phrase 2**: E F G G F E
- **Phrase 3**: G A G F E D
- **Phrase 4**: C D E D C

Fingering Instructions

Each note corresponds to a specific position on the slider. Here's a breakdown of where to place your finger for each note and how to move smoothly between them:

211

- **C Note**: Located near the bottom of the slider, closer to the base.
- **D Note**: Just above C, requiring a small upward slide.
- **E Note**: Slightly above D, about halfway up the slider.
- **F Note**: Just above E, requiring a slight upward slide.
- **G Note**: Closer to the middle of the slider.
- **A Note**: Slightly above G, requiring a gentle slide up.

Step-by-Step Instructions for Each Phrase

Phrase 1: C D E E D C

1. **Start on C**: Place your finger near the lower end of the slider and play C once.
2. **Slide Up to D**: Move your finger slightly up from C to reach D and play it once.
3. **Move Up to E**: Slide up further to reach E and play it twice with a steady rhythm.

4. **Slide Down to D**: Move back down to D and play it once.

5. **Return to C**: Slide down to C for the final note of the phrase.

- **Practice Tip**: This phrase has a gentle, rising and falling pattern. Focus on keeping each slide smooth and even, especially when moving between E, D, and C.

Phrase 2: E F G G F E

1. **Start on E**: Place your finger on E and play it once.

2. **Slide Up to F**: Move slightly up to reach F and play it once.

3. **Slide Up to G**: Continue moving up to G and play it twice.

4. **Slide Down to F**: Move back down to F and play it once.

5. **Return to E**: Slide down to E for the final note.

213

- **Practice Tip**: Focus on creating a smooth, connected sound as you slide up to G and then back down. Let the G notes resonate slightly to add warmth.

Phrase 3: G A G F E D

1. **Start on G**: Play G once.
2. **Slide Up to A**: Move slightly up to reach A and play it once.
3. **Return to G**: Slide back down to G and play it once.
4. **Slide Down to F**: Move down to F and play it once.
5. **Move Down to E**: Continue sliding down to E and play it once.
6. **Finish on D**: Slide down to D for the last note in the phrase.

- **Practice Tip**: This phrase has both ascending and descending movements. Work on keeping each slide connected,

214

especially the descending notes from G down to D.

Phrase 4: C D E D C

1. **Start on C**: Position your finger near the bottom of the slider and play C once.
2. **Slide Up to D**: Move up slightly to reach D and play it once.
3. **Slide Up to E**: Move up to E and play it once.
4. **Return to D**: Slide down to D and play it once.
5. **Finish on C**: Slide down to C for the final note, letting it resonate softly to close the song.

- **Practice Tip**: This final phrase has a gentle, descending feel. Focus on a smooth slide between D and C, and soften the last note to create a peaceful ending.

215

Practice Tips for "Lavender's Blue"

1. **Play with a Relaxed Tempo**: "Lavender's Blue" is a slow, flowing song. Use a metronome set to a slow tempo (around 50 BPM) to help keep each note steady and relaxed. This tempo allows you to focus on creating a smooth, connected sound.

2. **Practice Smooth Transitions**: Since the melody is gentle, practice sliding between notes without lifting your finger. This will help create a connected, flowing sound that captures the soothing nature of the song.

3. **Use Dynamics to Add Emotion**: Start each phrase softly, increase the volume slightly in the middle, and then soften at the end. These dynamics will give the song an expressive, emotional quality.

4. **Repeat Each Phrase for Consistency**: Practice each phrase individually until you're comfortable with the transitions and

note positions. This will help you play the full song with a consistent sound and smooth phrasing.

5. **Add Gentle Vibrato on Long Notes**: For added expressiveness, add a gentle vibrato on longer notes like G or E. Lightly pulse the "mouth" of the Otamatone to create a subtle vibrato effect that enhances the song's calming tone.

6. **Play with Feeling**: "Lavender's Blue" is a peaceful, soothing song. Take your time with each note and focus on creating a warm, resonant sound to capture the gentle character of the melody.

Song 22. "Camptown Races"

"Camptown Races" is an upbeat and rhythmic folk song with a lively melody. Its repetitive structure makes it approachable for beginners and provides a great opportunity to work on pitch accuracy, consistent timing, and smooth transitions on the Otamatone.

Notes and Phrases

- **Phrase 1**: C E G E C
- **Phrase 2**: D D E C D E C
- **Phrase 3**: C E G E C
- **Phrase 4**: D D E C D E C

Fingering Instructions

Here is a guide to locating each note on the Otamatone slider and moving smoothly between them:

- **C Note**: Near the lower end of the slider, closer to the base.
- **D Note**: Slightly above C, requiring a small slide up.
- **E Note**: Slightly above D, around the lower-middle section of the slider.

- **G Note**: Located around the middle of the slider.

Step-by-Step Instructions for Each Phrase

Phrase 1: C E G E C

1. **Start on C**: Place your finger near the bottom of the slider and play C once.
2. **Slide Up to E**: Move your finger up to reach E and play it once.
3. **Slide Up to G**: Move further up the slider to reach G and play it once.
4. **Return to E**: Slide back down to E and play it once.
5. **Return to C**: Slide down to C for the final note of the phrase.

- **Practice Tip**: This phrase has an ascending and descending motion. Focus on smooth slides between C, E, and G, keeping each note steady and rhythmic.

Phrase 2: D D E C D E C

1. **Start on D**: Place your finger slightly above C and play D twice with a steady rhythm.
2. **Slide Up to E**: Move up slightly to reach E and play it once.
3. **Slide Down to C**: Move down to C and play it once.
4. **Return to D**: Slide back up to D and play it once.
5. **Move Up to E**: Slide up to E again and play it once.
6. **Finish on C**: Slide down to C for the final note.

- **Practice Tip**: Focus on the repetitive rhythm of D and the smooth transitions between D, E, and C. Keep each note consistent in volume and timing to capture the rhythm of the melody.

Phrase 3: C E G E C

1. **Repeat Phrase 1**: Follow the same steps as in Phrase 1.

- **Practice Tip**: Since this phrase repeats, use it to reinforce your control and accuracy in sliding between C, E, and G. Aim for consistent timing and tone.

Phrase 4: D D E C D E C

1. **Repeat Phrase 2**: Follow the same steps as in Phrase 2.

- **Practice Tip**: This final phrase repeats the second one, so focus on keeping a lively, consistent rhythm as you slide between the notes. End with a strong, resonant C for a confident finish.

Practice Tips for "Camptown Races"

1. **Use a Moderate Tempo**: This song has an upbeat tempo, so try setting a metronome to a moderate pace, around 80 BPM. Let the rhythm guide your timing, and maintain a steady pace for each note.

2. **Emphasize Repetition**: "Camptown Races" has a repetitive structure, so focus on making each repeated phrase sound consistent in pitch, tone, and timing. This will create a smooth, flowing sound that matches the song's lively character.

3. **Work on Smooth Transitions**: Sliding between notes like C, D, and E without lifting your finger will create a connected sound. Practice keeping a light and controlled pressure as you move between each note.

4. **Add Dynamics for Energy**: To add expressiveness, vary your dynamics slightly

within each phrase. For example, start each phrase with a bit more emphasis on the first note, then soften slightly as you finish. This will add a lively, engaging feel to the melody.

5. **Practice Each Phrase Separately**: Begin by practicing each phrase individually. Once you're comfortable, try connecting them to play the entire song smoothly.

6. **Add Gentle Vibrato for Style**: Adding a slight vibrato on longer notes, like the final C in each phrase, can give the song a touch of character. Lightly pulse the "mouth" of the Otamatone to create a subtle vibrato effect, adding a bit of flair to your performance.

Song 23. "Alouette"

"Alouette" is a cheerful French folk song that's great for practicing rhythmic consistency, smooth note transitions, and dynamic control on the

Otamatone. Its repetitive structure and lively melody make it a fun and accessible song for beginners to learn.

Notes and Phrases

- **Phrase 1**: C D E C D E
- **Phrase 2**: G F E F G
- **Phrase 3**: C D E C D E
- **Phrase 4**: G F E D C

Fingering Instructions

Each note corresponds to a specific position on the Otamatone's slider. Here's where to locate each note and how to transition smoothly between them:

- **C Note**: Found near the lower end of the slider, close to the base.
- **D Note**: Slightly above C, requiring a small slide up.
- **E Note**: Higher up from D, closer to the lower-middle section of the slider.

- **F Note**: Just above E, slightly below G.
- **G Note**: Around the middle of the slider.

Step-by-Step Instructions for Each Phrase

Phrase 1: C D E C D E

1. **Start on C**: Place your finger near the bottom of the slider and play C once.
2. **Slide Up to D**: Move slightly up from C to reach D and play it once.
3. **Slide Up to E**: Move up further to reach E and play it once.
4. **Return to C**: Slide back down to C and play it once.
5. **Slide Up to D**: Move up again to D and play it once.
6. **Move Up to E**: Slide up to E and play it once more to complete the phrase.

- **Practice Tip**: Focus on keeping each slide smooth and steady, as this phrase repeats.

The rhythm should feel upbeat and consistent.

Phrase 2: G F E F G

1. **Start on G**: Position your finger around the middle of the slider and play G once.
2. **Slide Down to F**: Move your finger slightly down from G to reach F and play it once.
3. **Move Down to E**: Slide down further to E and play it once.
4. **Return to F**: Slide back up to F and play it once.
5. **Return to G**: Slide back up to G for the final note of the phrase.

- **Practice Tip**: This phrase moves up and down the slider, so work on maintaining control between G, F, and E. Focus on even timing to keep the rhythm lively.

Phrase 3: C D E C D E

1. **Repeat Phrase 1**: Follow the exact steps as in Phrase 1.

- **Practice Tip**: Use this repetition to reinforce accuracy and control in sliding between C, D, and E. Keep your timing consistent and focus on a smooth, connected sound.

Phrase 4: G F E D C

1. **Start on G**: Play G once with a steady tone.
2. **Slide Down to F**: Move slightly down to reach F and play it once.
3. **Slide Down to E**: Continue sliding down to E and play it once.
4. **Move Down to D**: Slide down further to D and play it once.
5. **Finish on C**: Slide down to C for the final note, letting it resonate to complete the song.

- **Practice Tip**: This final descending phrase provides a strong ending to the melody. Focus on keeping each transition smooth and steady, with a gentle finish on C.

Practice Tips for "Alouette"

1. **Use a Lively Tempo**: "Alouette" has an upbeat rhythm. Set a metronome to a moderate tempo (around 70-80 BPM) to help you keep a steady pace and bring out the song's lively character.

2. **Repeat for Consistency**: Since "Alouette" has repeated phrases, focus on making each repetition sound consistent in timing and tone. This will give the song a smooth, flowing sound and reinforce muscle memory.

3. **Work on Smooth Transitions**: Sliding between C, D, and E without lifting your finger will create a connected sound.

Practice keeping a light, controlled touch on the slider as you move between each note.

4. **Add Dynamics for Expression**: Vary the volume slightly within each phrase. For example, start each phrase with a strong note and then soften as you move through the melody. This adds expressiveness and energy to the song.

5. **Practice Each Phrase Separately**: Begin by practicing each phrase individually. Once you're comfortable, connect the phrases to play the full song smoothly.

6. **Use Gentle Vibrato for Style**: Add a gentle vibrato on longer notes, such as the final C in each phrase. Lightly pulse the Otamatone's "mouth" to create a subtle vibrato effect, giving the song a bit of extra flair.

Song 24. "Rock-a-Bye Baby"

"Rock-a-Bye Baby" is a soothing lullaby that's perfect for practicing smooth note transitions, gentle dynamics, and expressive control on the Otamatone. The slow tempo and flowing melody allow you to focus on creating a soft, connected sound.

Notes and Phrases

- **Phrase 1**: G E G C
- **Phrase 2**: D E F E D C
- **Phrase 3**: G E G C
- **Phrase 4**: D E F E D C

Fingering Instructions

Each note corresponds to a different position on the Otamatone's slider. Here's where to find each note and how to transition between them smoothly:

- **G Note**: Around the middle of the slider.

- **E Note**: Below G, closer to the lower-middle section of the slider.
- **C Note**: Near the lower end of the slider, close to the base.
- **D Note**: Just above C, requiring a slight upward slide.
- **F Note**: Slightly above E, between E and G.

Step-by-Step Instructions for Each Phrase

Phrase 1: G E G C

1. **Start on G**: Position your finger around the middle of the slider and play G once, letting it resonate softly.
2. **Slide Down to E**: Move your finger down to E and play it once.
3. **Return to G**: Slide back up to G and play it once more.
4. **Slide Down to C**: Move your finger down to C for the final note of the phrase.

231

- **Practice Tip**: Focus on creating a soft, smooth slide between each note. This phrase should feel gentle and connected, capturing the lullaby's calming mood.

Phrase 2: D E F E D C

1. **Start on D**: Place your finger just above C on the slider and play D once.
2. **Slide Up to E**: Move up slightly to reach E and play it once.
3. **Move Up to F**: Slide up to F and play it once.
4. **Return to E**: Slide back down to E and play it once.
5. **Slide Down to D**: Move down to D and play it once.
6. **Finish on C**: Slide down to C for the final note, allowing it to resonate softly.

- **Practice Tip**: This phrase has both ascending and descending notes. Practice keeping each slide smooth and gentle, especially as you transition down from F to C.

Phrase 3: G E G C

1. **Repeat Phrase 1**: Follow the same steps as in Phrase 1.

- **Practice Tip**: Since this phrase repeats, focus on keeping each slide consistent in tone and volume. Aim for a gentle, flowing sound.

Phrase 4: D E F E D C

1. **Repeat Phrase 2**: Follow the same steps as in Phrase 2.

- **Practice Tip**: This final phrase mirrors Phrase 2. Use it to reinforce smooth sliding between the notes, letting the final C resonate for a soft, peaceful ending.

Practice Tips for "Rock-a-Bye Baby"

1. **Play at a Slow, Relaxed Tempo**: "Rock-a-Bye Baby" is a lullaby, so use a metronome set to a slow tempo (around 50 BPM) to keep the pace gentle and relaxed. Take your time with each note, letting the song's peaceful character come through.

2. **Focus on Smooth Transitions**: Sliding smoothly between notes like G, E, and C is essential for creating a connected, flowing sound. Avoid lifting your finger between notes, keeping a light and steady pressure on the slider.

3. **Use Gentle Dynamics**: Start each phrase softly, increase the volume slightly in the middle, and then soften again at the end. This dynamic range will add emotional depth to the melody.

4. **Repeat Each Phrase for Consistency**: Practice each phrase individually to build

confidence in the transitions and note placements. This will help you play the full song with a consistent, soothing sound.

5. **Add Vibrato on Long Notes for Expression**: Adding a gentle vibrato on the final note in each phrase, such as C or G, can enhance the lullaby's calming effect. Lightly pulse the Otamatone's "mouth" to create a subtle vibrato, adding warmth and expressiveness to the melody.

6. **Play with Feeling**: This song is meant to be calming and comforting. Take your time with each note and focus on creating a warm, resonant sound that reflects the gentle nature of the lullaby.

Song 25. "Michael Row the Boat Ashore"

"Michael Row the Boat Ashore" is a traditional spiritual song with a gentle, flowing melody that's ideal for practicing smooth slides, expressive dynamics, and consistent timing on the Otamatone.

Its repetitive, calming rhythm provides a great way to focus on creating a connected, resonant sound.

Notes and Phrases

- **Phrase 1**: G E G E
- **Phrase 2**: G A G F E
- **Phrase 3**: E D C D E
- **Phrase 4**: G E D C

Fingering Instructions

Each note corresponds to a specific position on the Otamatone slider. Here's where to locate each note and how to transition smoothly between them:

- **G Note**: Around the middle of the slider.
- **E Note**: Below G, closer to the lower-middle section.
- **A Note**: Slightly above G, requiring a gentle upward slide.
- **F Note**: Just below G, between G and E.

- **D Note**: Lower than E, closer to the bottom of the slider.
- **C Note**: Near the lower end of the slider, close to the base.

Step-by-Step Instructions for Each Phrase

Phrase 1: G E G E

1. **Start on G**: Position your finger around the middle of the slider and play G once with a soft, steady tone.
2. **Slide Down to E**: Move your finger down to E and play it once.
3. **Return to G**: Slide back up to G and play it again.
4. **Return to E**: Slide back down to E for the final note of the phrase.

- **Practice Tip**: This phrase has a calm, repetitive feel. Focus on creating a smooth, controlled slide between G and E to capture the song's gentle rhythm.

Phrase 2: G A G F E

1. **Start on G**: Place your finger on G and play it once.
2. **Slide Up to A**: Move slightly up from G to reach A and play it once.
3. **Return to G**: Slide back down to G and play it again.
4. **Slide Down to F**: Move slightly down to F and play it once.
5. **Finish on E**: Slide down to E for the final note.

- **Practice Tip**: This phrase includes both upward and downward slides. Work on making each slide smooth and controlled, especially between G and A, then down to F and E.

Phrase 3: E D C D E

1. **Start on E**: Position your finger on E and play it once.

2. **Slide Down to D**: Move your finger down to D and play it once.

3. **Slide Down to C**: Move further down to reach C and play it once.

4. **Return to D**: Slide back up to D and play it once.

5. **Return to E**: Slide up to E for the final note.

- **Practice Tip**: This phrase has a descending and ascending pattern. Focus on smooth, connected slides as you move between each note.

Phrase 4: G E D C

1. **Start on G**: Place your finger on G and play it once.

2. **Slide Down to E**: Move your finger down to E and play it once.

3. **Slide Down to D**: Continue sliding down to D and play it once.

4. **Finish on C**: Slide down to C for the last note, letting it resonate softly to complete the song.

- **Practice Tip**: This final descending phrase brings the melody to a gentle close. Try softening the volume as you move from G to C for a peaceful ending.

Practice Tips for "Michael Row the Boat Ashore"

1. **Play at a Slow, Relaxed Tempo**: Set a metronome to a slow tempo (around 50 BPM) to help keep each note steady and calm. This song's gentle character should be reflected in a smooth, unhurried tempo.

2. **Focus on Smooth Transitions**: Sliding between notes without lifting your finger will help create a connected, flowing sound. Practice keeping your touch light and even as you move between each note.

3. **Use Dynamics for Expression**: Begin each phrase softly, build up slightly in the middle, and then soften again toward the end. This adds depth to the melody, enhancing the song's calming, spiritual quality.

4. **Repeat Each Phrase for Consistency**: Practice each phrase individually to build confidence in your note transitions and timing. Once you're comfortable with each part, connect them for a smooth, flowing melody.

5. **Add Gentle Vibrato on Long Notes**: Adding a gentle vibrato on the final note in each phrase, such as E or G, can enhance the song's soothing effect. Lightly pulse the

Otamatone's "mouth" to create a subtle vibrato that adds warmth and expression.

6. **Play with Feeling**: "Michael Row the Boat Ashore" has a reflective and soulful character. Take your time with each note and focus on creating a warm, resonant sound that conveys the song's peaceful nature.

Song 26. "Home on the Range"

"Home on the Range" is a classic American folk song with a gentle, flowing melody. Its smooth phrasing and moderate tempo make it a great choice for practicing pitch accuracy, dynamic control, and smooth slides on the Otamatone. The song's serene character provides an excellent opportunity to work on creating an expressive, connected sound.

Notes and Phrases

- **Phrase 1**: G E D E G
- **Phrase 2**: G A B G E
- **Phrase 3**: E G A B A G
- **Phrase 4**: E D C

Fingering Instructions

Each note corresponds to a specific position on the Otamatone slider. Here's how to locate each note and how to transition smoothly between them:

- **G Note**: Around the middle of the slider.
- **E Note**: Below G, in the lower-middle section.
- **D Note**: Slightly below E, closer to the lower end of the slider.
- **C Note**: Near the bottom of the slider, close to the base.
- **A Note**: Just above G, requiring a gentle upward slide.

243

- **B Note**: Higher up from A, slightly above the middle section of the slider.

Step-by-Step Instructions for Each Phrase

Phrase 1: G E D E G

1. **Start on G**: Position your finger around the middle of the slider and play G once with a soft, steady tone.
2. **Slide Down to E**: Move your finger down to E and play it once.
3. **Slide Down to D**: Move down to D and play it once.
4. **Return to E**: Slide back up to E and play it once.
5. **Return to G**: Slide up to G for the final note of the phrase.

- **Practice Tip**: This phrase has a gentle, rising and falling pattern. Focus on smooth slides and a consistent rhythm as you transition between G, E, and D.

Phrase 2: G A B G E

1. **Start on G**: Place your finger on G and play it once.
2. **Slide Up to A**: Move slightly up from G to reach A and play it once.
3. **Move Up to B**: Slide up further to B and play it once.
4. **Return to G**: Slide down to G and play it once.
5. **Finish on E**: Slide down to E for the final note of the phrase.

- **Practice Tip**: This phrase has an ascending and descending pattern. Try to maintain a smooth connection between each note, especially between A, B, and back to G.

Phrase 3: E G A B A G

1. **Start on E**: Position your finger on E and play it once.
2. **Slide Up to G**: Move up to G and play it once.
3. **Move Up to A**: Slide further up to reach A and play it once.
4. **Move Up to B**: Slide up slightly to reach B and play it once.
5. **Return to A**: Slide back down to A and play it once.
6. **Finish on G**: Slide down to G for the final note of the phrase.

- **Practice Tip**: Focus on smooth, consistent slides between G, A, and B, as this phrase has a balanced rise and fall. Try to keep each note even in timing.

Phrase 4: E D C

1. **Start on E**: Play E once with a steady tone.
2. **Slide Down to D**: Move your finger down to reach D and play it once.
3. **Finish on C**: Slide down to C for the final note, letting it resonate for a peaceful ending.

- **Practice Tip**: This closing phrase has a descending motion. Try to soften the volume as you slide from E to C for a calm, gentle finish.

Practice Tips for "Home on the Range"

1. **Play at a Moderate Tempo**: "Home on the Range" has a relaxed, steady tempo. Set a metronome to around 60 BPM to help keep each note even and steady. The rhythm should feel calm and flowing, reflecting the song's serene character.

2. **Focus on Smooth Transitions**: Since the melody is gentle, practice sliding between notes without lifting your finger. Keep a light and controlled touch on the slider to create a connected, flowing sound.

3. **Use Dynamics for Expression**: Add dynamics to each phrase. Start softly, build slightly in the middle, and then soften again toward the end. This dynamic range will add emotional depth and make the melody more engaging.

4. **Practice Each Phrase Individually**: Break the song down into phrases and practice each one separately to build confidence in note transitions and timing. Once you're comfortable, connect the phrases to play the full song smoothly.

5. **Add Gentle Vibrato on Long Notes**: For added expression, try adding a gentle vibrato to longer notes like the final G or C in each phrase. Lightly pulse the "mouth" of the

Otamatone to create a subtle vibrato, giving the song a warm, expressive feel.

6. **Play with Feeling**: "Home on the Range" has a nostalgic and reflective quality. Take your time with each note, focusing on creating a warm, resonant sound that captures the song's peaceful character.

Song 27. "The Farmer in the Dell"

"The Farmer in the Dell" is a playful nursery rhyme with a simple, repetitive melody. This song is excellent for beginners on the Otamatone to practice rhythm, smooth note transitions, and consistent timing. Its lively and repetitive structure makes it fun to learn and easy to remember.

Notes and Phrases

- **Phrase 1**: C C D E C
- **Phrase 2**: E F G
- **Phrase 3**: G A G F E

- **Phrase 4**: C E D C

Fingering Instructions

Here's a guide to locating each note on the Otamatone slider and how to transition smoothly between them:

- **C Note**: Near the lower end of the slider, close to the base.
- **D Note**: Slightly above C, requiring a small slide up.
- **E Note**: Above D, around the lower-middle section.
- **F Note**: Just above E.
- **G Note**: Around the middle of the slider.
- **A Note**: Slightly above G.

Step-by-Step Instructions for Each Phrase

Phrase 1: C C D E C

1. **Start on C**: Place your finger near the base of the slider and play C twice, keeping a steady rhythm.
2. **Slide Up to D**: Move your finger slightly up from C to reach D and play it once.
3. **Slide Up to E**: Continue moving up to reach E and play it once.
4. **Return to C**: Slide down to C for the final note.

- **Practice Tip**: Focus on the slide between C, D, and E. This phrase is upbeat, so keep your rhythm steady and lively.

Phrase 2: E F G

1. **Start on E**: Position your finger on E and play it once.

2. **Slide Up to F**: Move up slightly from E to reach F and play it once.

3. **Slide Up to G**: Move up further to reach G and play it once.

- **Practice Tip**: This phrase has an ascending pattern. Work on smooth slides between E, F, and G to create a connected sound.

Phrase 3: G A G F E

1. **Start on G**: Place your finger on G and play it once.

2. **Slide Up to A**: Move slightly up to reach A and play it once.

3. **Return to G**: Slide back down to G and play it once.

4. **Slide Down to F**: Move down to F and play it once.

5. **Return to E**: Slide down to E for the final note.

- **Practice Tip**: This phrase has both ascending and descending notes. Focus on the smooth transition between A, G, F, and E.

Phrase 4: C E D C

1. **Start on C**: Play C once with a clear tone.
2. **Slide Up to E**: Move your finger up to reach E and play it once.
3. **Slide Down to D**: Move slightly down from E to reach D and play it once.
4. **Return to C**: Slide back down to C for the final note, allowing it to resonate to end the song.

- **Practice Tip**: This final phrase has a mix of up-and-down slides. Practice each transition carefully, letting the final note (C) resonate softly.

Practice Tips for "The Farmer in the Dell"

1. **Use a Moderate, Lively Tempo**: "The Farmer in the Dell" is a cheerful song, so set a metronome to a moderate tempo (around 70-80 BPM). This will help keep the rhythm steady and give the melody a lively feel.

2. **Work on Consistent Repeated Notes**: In phrases with repeated notes like C in Phrase 1, focus on making each note sound even and consistent. This helps maintain the melody's structure and rhythm.

3. **Practice Smooth Transitions**: Sliding between notes like C, D, and E without lifting your finger will create a connected sound. Practice keeping a light, controlled touch on the slider as you move between each note.

4. **Add Dynamics for Expressiveness**: Try adding a bit of dynamic variation. Play the first note of each phrase slightly louder and

soften as you go. This can make the melody more engaging and give it a playful character.

5. **Practice Each Phrase Separately**: Begin by practicing each phrase individually to build confidence in timing and note accuracy. Once you feel comfortable, connect the phrases for a smooth performance.

6. **Play with a Happy, Light Touch**: "The Farmer in the Dell" is a playful tune. Keep a light, joyful touch as you play to capture the upbeat spirit of the song.

Song 28. "Scarborough Fair"

"Scarborough Fair" is a beautiful, haunting English folk song that's excellent for practicing expressive dynamics, smooth slides, and timing on the Otamatone. Its flowing melody provides a great opportunity to work on phrasing and creating a connected, resonant sound.

Notes and Phrases

- **Phrase 1**: G A B A G E
- **Phrase 2**: G A B D B A
- **Phrase 3**: G A B A G E
- **Phrase 4**: D B A G

Fingering Instructions

Each note corresponds to a specific position on the Otamatone slider. Here's where to locate each note and how to transition smoothly between them:

- **G Note**: Around the middle of the slider.
- **A Note**: Slightly above G.
- **B Note**: Higher up from A.
- **D Note**: Located above B, in the upper-middle part of the slider.
- **E Note**: Below G, closer to the lower-middle section.

Step-by-Step Instructions for Each Phrase

Phrase 1: G A B A G E

1. **Start on G**: Place your finger around the middle of the slider and play G once with a steady tone.
2. **Slide Up to A**: Move slightly up from G to reach A and play it once.
3. **Slide Up to B**: Move further up to reach B and play it once.
4. **Return to A**: Slide down to A and play it once.
5. **Return to G**: Slide down to G and play it once.
6. **Finish on E**: Slide down to E for the final note of the phrase.

- **Practice Tip**: This phrase has an ascending and descending flow. Focus on keeping each transition smooth and steady to capture the song's gentle rhythm.

257

Phrase 2: G A B D B A

1. **Start on G**: Play G once.
2. **Slide Up to A**: Move up to reach A and play it once.
3. **Slide Up to B**: Move further up to reach B and play it once.
4. **Slide Up to D**: Move up to D and play it once.
5. **Return to B**: Slide back down to B and play it once.
6. **Return to A**: Slide down to A for the final note.

- **Practice Tip**: This phrase reaches a higher note with D before descending back down. Focus on creating a connected, gentle sound, especially when moving between B, D, and back to A.

Phrase 3: G A B A G E

1. **Repeat Phrase 1**: Follow the same steps as in Phrase 1.

- **Practice Tip**: Since this phrase is a repetition, aim for consistency in tone and timing. Let each slide feel smooth and connected.

Phrase 4: D B A G

1. **Start on D**: Play D once with a steady, resonant tone.
2. **Slide Down to B**: Move down to B and play it once.
3. **Slide Down to A**: Move down to A and play it once.
4. **Finish on G**: Slide down to G for the final note, letting it resonate softly to end the song.

- **Practice Tip**: This descending phrase brings the melody to a close. Focus on a gentle, connected slide down to G, allowing the last note to resonate for a peaceful finish.

Practice Tips for "Scarborough Fair"

1. **Use a Slow, Steady Tempo**: "Scarborough Fair" has a reflective, calm melody. Set a metronome to a slow tempo (around 50 BPM) to keep each note steady and flowing. This tempo helps create a gentle, unhurried sound.

2. **Focus on Smooth Transitions**: Sliding between notes like G, A, and B without lifting your finger will help maintain a connected sound. Keep your touch light and controlled to make the melody sound continuous and resonant.

3. **Use Dynamics for Expression**: Start each phrase softly, build slightly in the middle, and soften again at the end. These dynamics

give the song emotional depth, enhancing its haunting, ethereal quality.

4. **Repeat Each Phrase for Consistency**: Practice each phrase individually to build confidence with the transitions and timing. This will allow you to play the song smoothly and expressively.

5. **Add Gentle Vibrato on Long Notes**: Try adding a slight vibrato on longer notes, such as D or G, to give the song extra warmth. Lightly pulse the Otamatone's "mouth" to create a subtle vibrato effect that adds expressiveness.

6. **Play with Feeling**: "Scarborough Fair" has a wistful, nostalgic feel. Take your time with each note and focus on creating a warm, resonant sound that conveys the song's emotional depth.

Song 29. "O Susanna"

"O Susanna" is a lively American folk song with a cheerful melody that's perfect for practicing rhythmic accuracy, smooth slides, and dynamic control on the Otamatone. Its upbeat tempo and repetitive structure make it a fun choice for beginners to build confidence and consistency.

Notes and Phrases

- **Phrase 1**: C E G E C
- **Phrase 2**: D D E C E G
- **Phrase 3**: C E G E C
- **Phrase 4**: D D E C D C

Fingering Instructions

Here's where to locate each note on the slider and how to transition smoothly between them:

- **C Note**: Near the lower end of the slider, close to the base.

- **D Note**: Slightly above C, requiring a small slide up.
- **E Note**: Just above D, in the lower-middle section.
- **G Note**: Located around the middle of the slider.

Step-by-Step Instructions for Each Phrase

Phrase 1: C E G E C

1. **Start on C**: Place your finger near the base of the slider and play C once.
2. **Slide Up to E**: Move your finger up to reach E and play it once.
3. **Slide Up to G**: Move up to G and play it once.
4. **Return to E**: Slide down to E and play it once.
5. **Return to C**: Slide down to C for the final note.

- **Practice Tip**: Focus on keeping each slide smooth and rhythmic, especially the slide up from C to G and back. Aim for a lively, cheerful sound to capture the song's spirit.

Phrase 2: D D E C E G

1. **Start on D**: Slide slightly up from C to reach D and play it twice with even timing.
2. **Slide Up to E**: Move up to E and play it once.
3. **Slide Down to C**: Move back down to C and play it once.
4. **Return to E**: Slide up to E and play it once.
5. **Finish on G**: Slide up to G for the final note.

- **Practice Tip**: This phrase includes both repeated and ascending notes. Work on keeping each note even in timing to maintain a steady rhythm.

Phrase 3: C E G E C

1. **Repeat Phrase 1**: Follow the same steps as in Phrase 1.

- **Practice Tip**: Since this phrase repeats, focus on making it sound consistent. Use this repetition to solidify your rhythm and accuracy.

Phrase 4: D D E C D C

1. **Start on D**: Play D twice with a steady rhythm.
2. **Slide Up to E**: Move up to E and play it once.
3. **Slide Down to C**: Move your finger down to C and play it once.
4. **Return to D**: Slide up to D and play it once.
5. **Finish on C**: Slide down to C for the final note, letting it resonate for a confident ending.

- **Practice Tip**: This phrase has a descending pattern. Focus on keeping each slide smooth and connected, letting the last C ring out to complete the melody.

Practice Tips for "O Susanna"

1. **Use a Steady, Lively Tempo**: "O Susanna" has an upbeat feel. Set a metronome to a moderate tempo (around 80-90 BPM) to keep each note steady and energetic.

2. **Emphasize Repeated Notes**: In phrases like Phrase 2, with repeated Ds, focus on keeping each note consistent in tone and timing. This will help the song maintain its rhythmic character.

3. **Work on Smooth Transitions**: Sliding between notes like C, D, and E without lifting your finger will create a connected sound. Practice keeping your touch light and steady as you move between each note.

4. **Add Dynamics for Expression**: Use dynamics to enhance the lively feel of the song. Try playing the first note of each phrase slightly louder and softening as you move through the melody to add a cheerful, playful quality.

5. **Practice Each Phrase Individually**: Break the song down into phrases and practice each one separately to build confidence in note accuracy and timing. Once you're comfortable, connect the phrases for a smooth performance.

6. **Use Vibrato on Long Notes for Emphasis**: For extra style, add a gentle vibrato to longer notes, such as the final C in each phrase. Lightly pulse the Otamatone's "mouth" to create a subtle vibrato effect that enhances the song's lively character.

Song 30. "Are You Sleeping"

"Are You Sleeping" (also known as "Frère Jacques") is a simple and repetitive melody that is perfect for beginners. This song is great for practicing smooth transitions, rhythm, and consistent timing on the Otamatone. Its calm, flowing melody makes it easy to learn and enjoyable to play.

Notes and Phrases

- **Phrase 1**: C D E C
- **Phrase 2**: C D E C
- **Phrase 3**: E F G
- **Phrase 4**: E F G
- **Phrase 5**: G A G F E C
- **Phrase 6**: G A G F E C

Fingering Instructions

Here's where each note is located on the slider and how to transition smoothly between them:

- **C Note**: Near the lower end of the slider, close to the base.

- **D Note**: Slightly above C, requiring a small upward slide.

- **E Note**: Higher up from D, around the lower-middle section of the slider.

- **F Note**: Just above E, slightly below the middle.

- **G Note**: Around the middle of the slider.

- **A Note**: Slightly above G, requiring a small slide up.

Step-by-Step Instructions for Each Phrase

Phrase 1: C D E C

1. **Start on C**: Place your finger near the base of the slider and play C once with a steady tone.

2. **Slide Up to D**: Move your finger slightly up to reach D and play it once.

3. **Slide Up to E**: Move up further to reach E and play it once.

4. **Return to C**: Slide down to C for the final note of the phrase.

- **Practice Tip**: This phrase has a gentle, ascending and descending flow. Focus on smooth slides and keeping the timing even.

Phrase 2: C D E C

1. **Repeat Phrase 1**: Follow the same steps as in Phrase 1.

- **Practice Tip**: Since this phrase repeats, aim for consistency in tone and timing. Let each slide feel smooth and connected.

Phrase 3: E F G

1. **Start on E**: Place your finger on E and play it once.

2. **Slide Up to F**: Move slightly up from E to reach F and play it once.

3. **Slide Up to G**: Move up further to reach G and play it once.

- **Practice Tip**: This ascending phrase should feel smooth and flowing. Practice the gradual slide from E to G, keeping the rhythm steady.

Phrase 4: E F G

1. **Repeat Phrase 3**: Follow the same steps as in Phrase 3.

- **Practice Tip**: Use this repetition to reinforce accuracy and control in moving up the slider from E to G.

Phrase 5: G A G F E C

1. **Start on G**: Place your finger on G and play it once.

271

2. **Slide Up to A**: Move slightly up to reach A and play it once.

3. **Return to G**: Slide back down to G and play it once.

4. **Slide Down to F**: Move down to F and play it once.

5. **Slide Down to E**: Continue sliding down to E and play it once.

6. **Finish on C**: Slide down to C for the final note of the phrase.

- **Practice Tip**: This phrase combines ascending and descending notes. Practice each transition carefully, especially the descending slides from G to C.

Phrase 6: G A G F E C

1. **Repeat Phrase 5**: Follow the same steps as in Phrase 5.

- **Practice Tip**: This final phrase mirrors Phrase 5, so use it to reinforce your control over the descending transitions, letting the final C resonate softly.

Practice Tips for "Are You Sleeping"

1. **Play at a Slow, Relaxed Tempo**: "Are You Sleeping" is a gentle song. Use a metronome set to a slow tempo (around 60 BPM) to help keep each note even and steady, allowing you to focus on creating a calm, flowing melody.

2. **Focus on Smooth Transitions**: Sliding between notes without lifting your finger will help maintain a connected sound. Keep your touch light and controlled to make the melody sound continuous.

3. **Use Dynamics for Expression**: Start each phrase softly, build slightly in the middle, and soften again at the end. These dynamics

add warmth to the melody and make it more expressive.

4. **Repeat Each Phrase for Consistency**: Practice each phrase individually to build confidence with the transitions and timing. This will allow you to play the song smoothly and with a gentle flow.

5. **Add Gentle Vibrato on Long Notes**: Adding a gentle vibrato to longer notes, such as G or C, can enhance the song's calming effect. Lightly pulse the Otamatone's "mouth" to create a subtle vibrato that adds expressiveness.

6. **Play with Feeling**: "Are You Sleeping" has a peaceful, lullaby quality. Take your time with each note and focus on creating a warm, resonant sound to capture the song's gentle character.

Chapter 8: Ear Training And Playing By Ear

Ear training is a crucial skill for any musician, helping develop the ability to recognize notes, intervals, and melodies without visual aids. By practicing ear training, you'll improve your musical intuition and develop the ability to play songs by ear on the Otamatone.

Introduction To Ear Training

What is Ear Training? Ear training is the practice of recognizing and identifying notes, intervals (the distance between two notes), and rhythms through listening. This skill enables musicians to identify melodies, reproduce them on an instrument, and even improvise without needing to read sheet music.

Why is Ear Training Important?

- **Develops Musical Memory**: Ear training helps build your internal "sound library" of notes and chords, making it easier to recall and reproduce melodies.

- **Improves Tuning and Pitch Accuracy**: You'll develop a stronger sense of pitch, making it easier to play in tune.
- **Enhances Confidence**: As you become familiar with notes and intervals by ear, you'll feel more confident when playing without music notation.
- **Enables Playing by Ear**: Eventually, ear training enables you to pick up songs on the Otamatone (or other instruments) just by listening.

Basic Ear Training Exercises

Start with these foundational exercises to develop pitch recognition and familiarize yourself with common intervals:

1. **Single-Note Matching**

- Listen to a note, then try to match it on the Otamatone slider. Start with a known note like G or C.
- Try playing the same note at different octaves to train your ear to hear pitch differences.

2. **Interval Recognition**
   - An interval is the distance between two notes. Practice recognizing common intervals such as a whole step (e.g., C to D) or a half step (e.g., E to F).
   - Play one note, then slide up or down to the next note in the interval. Over time, aim to recognize these intervals without using the slider.

3. **Simple Melody Recognition**
   - Start by listening to a short melody of two to three notes, like "Hot Cross Buns" (E D C), then try to reproduce it on the Otamatone by ear.

- Focus on the direction of each note (up or down) and the size of each interval (small or large).

Playing Simple Songs by Ear

Playing by ear involves finding each note in a melody without seeing written music. Start with familiar tunes and work gradually toward more complex songs as your ear improves.

Tips for Playing by Ear:

1. **Start with Simple Melodies**: Begin with songs that have clear, repetitive patterns, such as nursery rhymes ("Mary Had a Little Lamb") or folk tunes ("Twinkle, Twinkle Little Star").
2. **Break Down the Melody**: Instead of trying to find the whole song at once, break it down into short phrases of two to three notes.

3. **Identify Direction and Distance**:

   o **Direction**: After playing the first note, listen to whether the next note sounds higher or lower.

   o **Distance**: Estimate whether the interval is small (e.g., one step away like C to D) or larger (e.g., two steps away like C to E).

4. **Use Trial and Error**: Finding the exact notes may take several tries. Use this time to experiment and develop intuition without worrying about mistakes.

5. **Rely on Repetition**: Once you identify a phrase, repeat it until it feels natural. Then move on to the next phrase in the song.

Interactive Exercise: Simple Tunes for Ear Training

Try these easy, recognizable tunes as practice for playing by ear. Focus on identifying each note by sound rather than looking at notation.

1. **"Hot Cross Buns"** (E D C)
   - Start on E, then slide down to D, and then down to C. Listen carefully to the descending notes and focus on the change in pitch as you move down.
2. **"Mary Had a Little Lamb"** (E D C D E E E)
   - Begin on E, then slide down to D, down to C, and back up to D and E. Try to reproduce the melody by finding each note based on its pitch direction and distance.
3. **"Twinkle, Twinkle Little Star"** (C C G G A A G)

- Play C twice, then slide up to G twice, and up to A twice before returning to G. Listen to the larger intervals in this song as you work through each section.

4. **"Happy Birthday"** (G G A G C B)
   - Start on G, then move up to A, and repeat G, C, and B. Pay attention to the differences in pitch distance to find the notes accurately.

Developing Your Ear Training Routine

Ear training, like any other skill, improves with consistent practice. Set aside a few minutes each day to work on the exercises listed above, and try to incorporate listening practice into your music sessions. As you continue, you'll notice improvements in your ability to find notes, recognize intervals, and even identify the key of songs by ear.

Advancing Beyond Basic Ear Training

As you become comfortable with these exercises, you can expand ear training by:

- **Listening to Songs Without Your Instrument**: Try identifying notes and intervals just by listening.
- **Learning the Intervals for Each Key**: Practice playing intervals within different keys to reinforce pitch accuracy.
- **Practicing with a Partner**: Take turns with a partner playing notes or simple melodies for each other to identify by ear.

Chapter 9: Exploring Advanced Techniques

Double Stops And Harmonies

What Are Double Stops?

- Double stops involve playing two notes simultaneously or in quick succession to create a harmony. This technique adds richness to the melody and can be used to create chords or harmonies.

Producing Harmonies on the Otamatone

- Since the Otamatone is typically played one note at a time, true double stops are challenging to achieve. However, you can simulate harmonies by:
  - **Alternating between Two Notes Quickly**: Move your finger back and forth between two adjacent notes (e.g., C and E or G and B) to create a harmonic effect.

- **Using a Split Rhythm**: Alternate between two notes in a pattern that mimics a harmony, such as playing G and B in a "call-and-response" pattern.
- **Playing Notes in Close Succession**: Play one note immediately after the other, letting the ear perceive the harmony.

Tips for Creating Harmonies

1. **Choose Simple Intervals**: Start with thirds and fifths, such as C and E or C and G, as these intervals create stable, pleasing harmonies.
2. **Use Consistent Timing**: For a smooth effect, play the notes with an even rhythm, alternating between the two with a steady tempo.
3. **Experiment with Different Intervals**: Try varying intervals, such as fourths and sixths,

to add unique harmonic textures to your sound.

Octave Jumps and Positioning Tips

What Are Octave Jumps?

- An octave jump means playing the same note at a different pitch level, typically either one octave higher or lower. For example, moving from C in one octave to C in the next octave creates an octave jump. This technique adds dramatic effect and dynamic contrast to your playing.

Executing Octave Jumps on the Otamatone

1. **Learn the Position of Octaves on the Slider**: Familiarize yourself with where each octave of the notes C, D, E, etc., falls on the slider. This will help you confidently perform octave jumps without searching for the note each time.

2. **Use Reference Points**: Start by finding and memorizing key points along the slider for C, G, and A in different octaves. Use these reference notes as anchor points.

3. **Adjust Your Finger Placement**: Octave jumps require a precise adjustment of finger placement to move smoothly from one octave to the other. Practice shifting your finger in one quick motion without hesitating.

Tips for Mastering Octave Jumps

- **Start with Slow Octave Shifts**: Begin by playing a note in a low octave, then sliding up the slider to the higher octave slowly to get used to the distance.

- **Practice with a Metronome**: Set a metronome to a slow pace and practice jumping between octaves in time with the beat, gradually increasing the speed as you become more comfortable.

- **Combine with Dynamics**: Use a softer touch on lower octaves and a stronger touch on higher octaves to add dramatic effect to the octave jumps.

Exercise: Practicing Octave Shifts and Transitioning Between Harmonies

This exercise will help you combine octave jumps and harmony transitions to add expressive layers to your playing.

1. **Octave Jump Practice**
   - **Start on G (Low Octave)**: Begin by playing a G in the lower octave. Then quickly move your finger up to play G in the higher octave. Practice this shift until you can achieve it in one smooth motion.
   - **Repeat with C and D**: Practice jumping between low and high

octaves for C and D, as these notes
are often used in melodic transitions.

- ○ **Increase Speed Gradually**: Once
  you feel comfortable with the jump at
  a slow pace, increase the speed
  slightly to make the jump more
  natural and fluid.

2. **Transitioning Between Harmonies**

- ○ **Start with Third Intervals**: Choose
  an interval such as C and E. Play C
  first, then quickly move to E to create
  a harmony. Practice alternating
  between the two.

- ○ **Move to Fifth Intervals**: Now, try
  transitioning between C and G to
  create a fifth interval harmony.
  Alternate between these two notes
  smoothly.

- ○ **Combine Harmonies with Octave
  Jumps**: Start on a low C, play a
  harmony with G in the same octave,

then jump to a higher C and repeat the harmony with the higher G. This exercise will help you practice both transitions.

3. **Combining Octave Jumps and Harmonic Transitions in a Melody**

   o **Choose a Simple Tune**: Select a simple melody like "Twinkle, Twinkle, Little Star."

   o **Add Octave Jumps**: Add an octave jump every time the melody repeats a note, like moving from a lower C to a higher C.

   o **Incorporate Harmonies**: Add harmonies by alternating between intervals (like C and G) as you move through the melody, creating a fuller sound.

Advanced Tips for Double Stops, Octave Jumps, and Harmonies

1. **Use Vibrato for Emphasis**: Add a slight vibrato to longer notes in your harmony or octave jumps for a richer, more expressive sound.

2. **Combine with Dynamics**: Start each octave jump softly, then increase volume in the higher octave to add contrast. Similarly, emphasize the first note of a harmony, then soften the second.

3. **Experiment with Phrasing**: Try playing the melody with pauses between octave jumps and harmonies to create musical phrasing and give each section of the song character.

Made in the USA
Las Vegas, NV
23 December 2024

15208322R00164